the fish cookbook

Easy-to-use recipes
for tasty fish favourites

ROZ DENNY

MARTIN BOOKS

CONTENTS

NOTES
Ingredients are given in both metric and imperial measures. Use either set of quantities but not a mixture of both in any one recipe.

All spoon measurements are level:
1 tablespoon = one 15 ml spoon
1 teaspoon = one 5 ml spoon
Eggs are standard size 3 unless otherwise stated.

Published by Martin Books
Simon & Schuster International Group
Fitzwilliam House
32 Trumpington Street
Cambridge CB2 1QY

In association with the
Sea Fish Industry Authority
Sea Fisheries House
10 Young Street
Edinburgh EH2 4JQ

First published 1988

ISBN 0 85941 555 4

INTRODUCTION

With the healthy food revolution that has taken place over the last few years, and the increase in demand for high-protein, low-fat, quick-cook foods, it is no wonder that fish is enjoying something of a revival of interest. There are literally dozens of varieties to choose from, and lots of ways of cooking them. It's certainly easy to ring the changes with fish on your weekly family menu plan.

FEEDING FISH TO YOUR FAMILY

The biggest concern that many people have about eating fish is avoiding skin and bones. However, fishmongers are paying greater attention to preparing fish that can be popped straight into a pan once unwrapped in the home. Fish is increasingly being sold filleted, skinned and cut into attractive chunks of tasty, tempting goodness.

GROWING UP WITH FISH

Much of children's reluctance to eat fish probably stems from the fact that they aren't used to it. Yet white fish is an ideal food to wean babies on, and if introduced to it from the start they will soon take it for granted. It is tender, easy to chew and digest, quick to cook and, above all, tasty.

Introduce babies to white fish when they are about 6 months old, cooking it by poaching (unseasoned) in boiled water or baby milk, adding finely diced root vegetables, rice, potatoes or baby cereal and then blending to a fine purée. Allow about 25 g (1 oz) portion of fish per meal, but do take great care to check thoroughly for bones. Oily fish, such as herring and mackerel (again well boned), can be introduced to babies at about 8 months, cooking as above. However, around this age babies like a little texture in their food, so flake the fish well instead of puréeing it. Don't give cured (salted) and smoked fish to babies until they are about 18 months old.

Children tend to have somewhat conservative tastes, and it is therefore worth concentrating on serving fish in ways that they like. Cook white fish – such as plaice – in crunchy, tasty, crisp coatings, or serve in creamy-smooth sauces. Mix fish into their favourite meals, such as macaroni cheese and pies; and don't forget the traditionally popular fish 'n' chips. Finally, give these dishes catchy names, or name them in honour of your children. You will soon have clean plates and requests for more.

WHY FISH IS GOOD FOR US

No doubt we were all told as children that fish was good for us. Well, it really is! For a start it contains lots of high quality protein, practically no carbohydrate and fat, and yet white fish is low in calories. It is also a good source of minerals, containing iodine and fluorine needed for the body's metabolism, and calcium needed for growth and strong bones. All fish contain vitamins of the B group as well, including thiamin, riboflavin, niacin, B_6 and B_{12}. Most oily fish also contain lots of vitamin D, necessary for strong bones, and vitamin A, necessary for good eyesight and healthy skin.

In addition, white fish, such as cod and plaice, contain only a small amount of fat, less than 2%, with lots of water and virtually no carbohydrates. In fact, a 100 g (3½ oz) portion of white fish has only 80–90 calories, which makes it an ideal high-protein, slimming food. Oily fish vary considerably in fat content, depending on the time of the year and whether they have spawned or not. In spring the fat content of herring or mackerel may be as low as 5%, this can rise to 20% in summer or early autumn. The fat content of shellfish varies also, according to species, but most are low in fat and therefore low in calories, too. In addition to this, the fat found in fish is mainly of the unsaturated type and there is evidence to suggest that the fatty acids found in fish oils assist in preventing coronary heart disease.

Finally, fish does not lose its nutritional value once frozen. In fact there is very little nutritional difference between fresh and frozen fish. So, if you find it more convenient to use frozen fish, carry on.

BUYING FISH

When buying fish these are the points to look for:

Whole fish

● clear bright eyes ● shiny colourful skin ● firm flesh ● fresh sea smell

White fish fillets

● neat, trim shape ● white translucent appearance

Smoked fish

● fresh smoky aroma ● neat, firm fillets ● glossy appearance

Shellfish

● shells should be undamaged and closed tightly, without cracks ● should be heavy in weight, for their size

Frozen fish

● undamaged packaging ● no freezer burn, which has a greyish-white, dried-out appearance ● frozen hard, with no signs of thawing

STORING FISH

Fresh fish should be cleaned, rinsed in cold water and then patted dry with kitchen towel. Cover loosely with foil or cling film, or place in a polythene bag. Store towards the bottom of the fridge for a short time, certainly no longer than 2 days.

Smoked fish which is sold 'loose' should be eaten within 3 days when stored in a fridge. Vacuum-packed fish will have a 'sell by' date, so follow its recommendation.

Frozen fish will be marked with storage instructions on the packet, which should be followed correctly for the best eating quality.

If you do store frozen fish past its maximum date it won't be dangerous, just drier and not as pleasant to eat. It can still be used in saucy dishes or made into fish cakes. However, it is important to use oily fish, such as kippers, within the given storage date because of the fat content. Overlong storage may leave the fish with an unpleasant flavour.

MICROWAVING FISH

Fish is ideal for cooking in a microwave. It retains its flavour and texture and can be quickly and easily cooked with less risk of overcooking than when using conventional heat. Choose pieces of fish that are of an even thickness for the best results. Spread them out on a plate and brush with butter or oil. Sprinkle with lemon juice, herbs or spices and cover with microwave cling film, piercing a few times to allow steam to escape. Whole fish, such as herring or mackerel, should be slashed a couple of times on each side before cooking.

Check your recipe or microwave handbook for exact times and power, as this varies according to the output of your oven. Season after cooking and allow to stand for a couple of minutes before serving.

DIFFERENT KINDS OF FISH

There are several main groups of fish; here are some examples of the most popular fish within the most common groups:

Round white fish – cod, coley, haddock, conger eel, sea bass, hake, John Dory, ling, whiting, pollack, bream, grey/red mullet, monkfish

Flat white fish – plaice, dab, lemon sole, Dover sole, megrim, halibut, brill, turbot, witch

Oily fish – herring, mackerel, sprat, sardines, tuna

Cartilaginous fish – huss, skate, shark

Shellfish – crab, cockles, Dublin Bay prawn, mussels, shrimp, prawn, squid, scallops

SMOKED FISH

Nowadays, most smoked fish is made using very light smoking techniques, which cause no significant change in the nutrients. This lighter smoking also gives a milder flavour than traditional smoking, which more people seem to like, and often no dyes are used which gives a paler colour. However, if you prefer it, smoked fish with a stronger colour is still available.

There are two methods of smoking:

A. *'Cold' smoking* – where fish is cured by smoking at an air temperature not higher than 33°C, to avoid cooking the fish. These products should be cooked before eating, e.g. kippers.

B. *'Hot' smoking* – where fish is smoked at a temperature of 70°–80°C at some stage during the process, to cook the flesh. No further home-cooking is necessary, e.g. mackerel.

HOW TO PREPARE FISH

Boning herring and mackerel

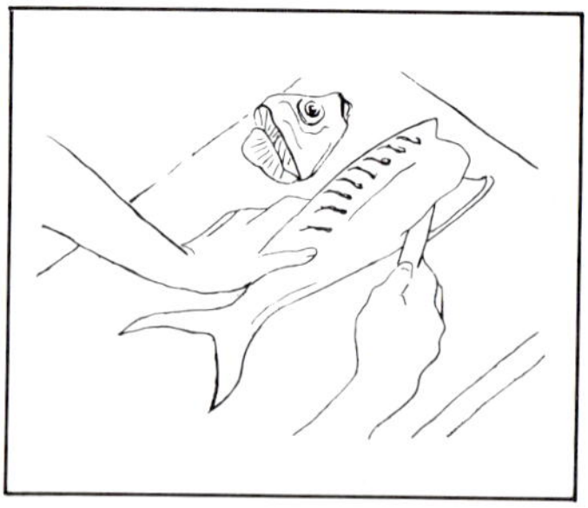

1. Using scissors, cut off the fins and cut just behind the gills to remove the head. Slit the fish along the belly and scoop away the insides, using kitchen towel.

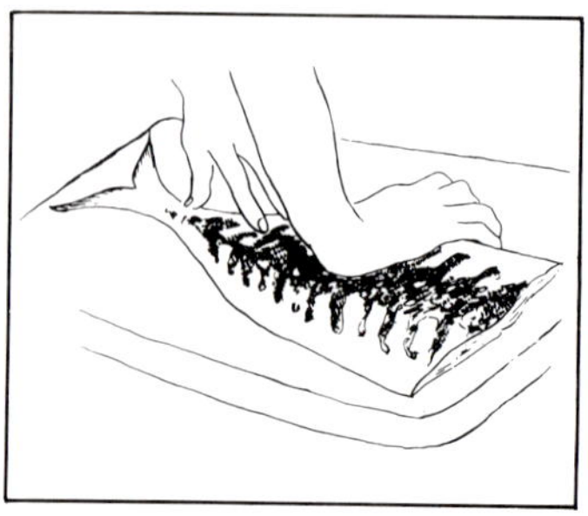

2. Open up the fish to the tail, and place skin uppermost on a board. Press firmly along the back of the fish, using your thumbs or the heel of your hand.

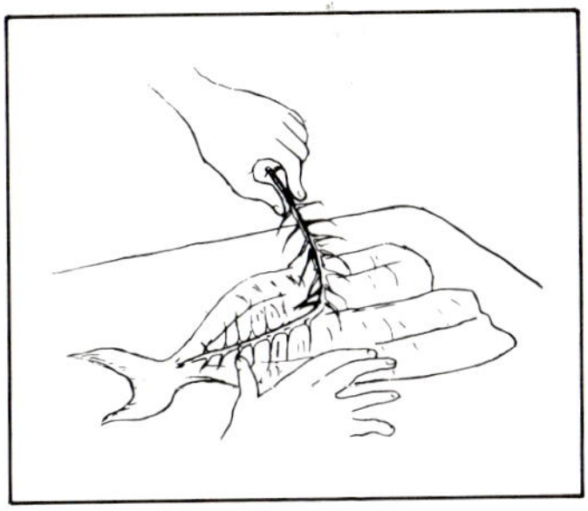

3. Turn the fish over and ease the backbone away from the flesh, cutting off at the tail. Rinse the fish and pat dry.

Removing the pin bones

These are found just underneath the gill fins in round fish. They can be removed easily before or after cooking.

1. Make a cut at a slight angle on each side of the line of bones. Remove the small, V-shaped piece of flesh, together with the bones.

Skinning fillets of flat or round fish

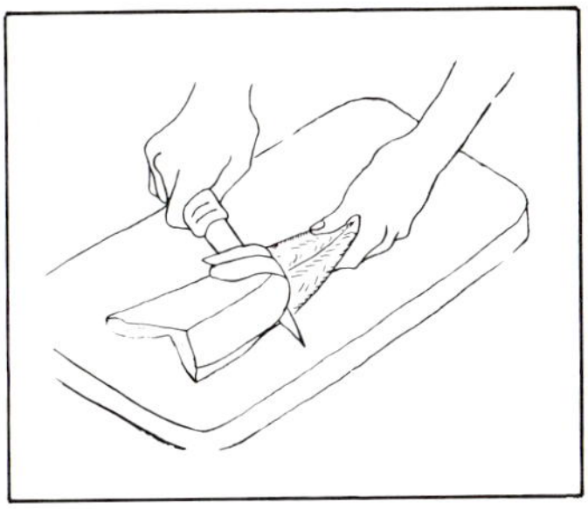

Fingers dipped in salt will help you keep a grip on the skin.

1. Place the fillet skin-side down, tail towards you. Make a 1 cm (½-inch) snip into the flesh at the tail end, and then insert your knife. Holding the tail skin, work the knife in a sawing action, slicing the flesh away from the skin. Hold the knife at an acute angle to the skin and keep the skin taut.

Thanks to my two daughters Felicity and Clemmie, aged 10 and 7, who munched their way through these recipes with few complaints.

Thanks, also, to consultant nutritionist Jenny Salmon, for her help with information in this introduction.

Roz Denny

Brunches and Snacks

Traditionally, the day started with a meal full of flavour, such as Finnan haddock, kippers or herring. These days, however, cooked breakfasts have been replaced by cereals and quickly prepared foods. Why not introduce the traditional family dishes in the form of brunch or snacks at weekends or holidays when there is more time to enjoy the first meal of the day, even if it is at 10.30 in the morning!

Brunch Club Sandwiches

These are ideal for taking out on to your patio on a sunny weekend morning.

SERVES 2–4

4 thin slices of back bacon, de-rinded
6 slices of wholemeal bread
1 large tomato, sliced thinly
a knob of butter or margarine, plus extra for spreading (optional)
2 eggs, beaten
125–175 g (4–6 oz) cooked and flaked smoked fish, e.g. haddock, kipper or cod
1 tablespoon chopped fresh parsley or chives
salt and freshly ground black pepper
4 stuffed olives, to garnish

1. Grill the bacon on both sides until just cooked.
2. Lightly toast the bread and then spread thinly with butter or margarine, if liked. Divide the bacon between two of the slices of toast; then top with the tomato and one more slice of toast each.
3. Melt a knob of butter or margarine in a small saucepan and, when it stops foaming, stir in the eggs. Season lightly and then add the fish. Stir to scramble lightly, taking care not to overcook.
4. Pile the egg and fish mixture immediately onto the sandwiches and scatter over the parsley or chives. Top with a final slice of toast each and cut both sandwiches in half diagonally. Serve as soon as possible, each one skewered with a cocktail stick and topped with an olive.

Top *Brunch Club Sandwiches*, below *White Fish Kromeskies*

White Fish Kromeskies

These consist of a tasty fish and egg filling, which is wrapped in bacon and then covered in a delicious crispy coating. They are great for a special brunch. They can be prepared the night before, just bake them in the oven in the morning.

MAKES 16

250 g (8 oz) white fish fillets, fresh or defrosted
300 ml (½ pint) milk
1 small carrot, quartered
1 bay leaf
1 fairly small onion, chopped
40 g (1½ oz) butter or margarine
125 g (4 oz) button mushrooms, chopped
40 g (1½ oz) flour
2 eggs, hard-boiled and chopped
50 g (2 oz) toasted hazelnuts, chopped (optional)
16 slices of back bacon, de-rinded and streaky end removed
salt and freshly ground black pepper
FOR THE COATING:
plain flour, to coat
2 eggs, beaten
about 175 g (6 oz) dried natural breadcrumbs
oil, for deep-fat frying

1. Place the fish, milk, carrot, bay leaf and a little of the onion in a saucepan. Season well and simmer gently for about 7 minutes. Allow to stand for 15 minutes after this. Then remove the fish, skin it and flake the flesh. Strain the milk and reserve, discarding the vegetables and flavourings.
2. In the same saucepan, melt the butter or margarine and gently sauté the rest of the onion and the mushrooms for about 3 minutes. Stir in the flour, cook for a minute and gradually blend in the strained milk.
3. Bring to the boil, stirring continuously until it has thickened; cook for another minute. The sauce should be quite thick.
4. Check the seasoning; then stir in the flaked fish, hard-boiled egg and toasted nuts, if using. Cool and then chill.
5. Divide the mixture into 16 portions and place one portion on each bacon rasher. Roll up each of these and place join-side down on a plate, ready for coating.
6. Have ready three small bowls: one containing the flour, one the beaten egg and one the breadcrumbs. Dip the rolls first in the flour and then in the egg, finally coat well in the breadcrumbs. Leave them uncovered in the fridge, until ready to deep-fry.
7. Fill a deep-fat frying pan a third full of oil and heat to a temperature of 185°C/360°F, or until a cube of day-old bread

browns in 30 seconds. Deep-fry the kromeskies in batches of four or five, for about 4 minutes each, until they are golden brown. Drain and keep each batch warm as you do this. Serve them hot with a spicy tomato relish.

Note: If you wish to reduce the amount of oil absorbed, deep-fry the kromeskies for a minute only, just to seal the outside. Then drain and bake in the oven, at Gas Mark 6/200°C/400°F, for about 20 minutes.

DEEP-FAT FRYING

Deep-fat frying is a delicious way of cooking fish but it can be quite dangerous, so always take care. Never leave a pan on the heat unattended; watch carefully to see that it doesn't boil over. Don't let children near the pan, and NEVER let a child do any deep-fat frying.

CHEESY FISH MUFFINS

Muffins are always popular with children, and these are almost pizza-style, which should appeal even more.

SERVES 2–4

2 muffins, split in half
butter or margarine, to spread (optional)
250 g (8 oz) skinned white fish fillets or 2 frozen fish steaks each weighing 100 g (3½ oz)
2 teaspoons lemon juice
1 large tomato, quartered, de-seeded and chopped roughly
50 g (2 oz) Cheddar or Edam cheese, grated
a large pinch of curry powder or dried thyme
salt and freshly ground black pepper

1. Lightly toast the muffins and then spread with butter or margarine, if liked.
2. Meanwhile, place the fish fillets or steaks on a grill pan, sprinkle them with the lemon juice and season well. Grill the fish for 5 minutes each side; then flake.
3. Mix this with the tomato and then pile onto the four muffin halves. Top each with the grated cheese and sprinkle over the curry powder or thyme.
4. Return to the grill and cook until the cheese is just beginning to bubble and turn golden brown. Eat as soon as possible.

Golden Fish with Poached Sunny Eggs

The simplest dishes are often the most popular and this dish – combining the creaminess of softly poached eggs with the full flavour of smoked fish – is no exception.

SERVES 4

3 bay leaves
a slice of lemon (optional)
a few blades of mace (optional)
750 g (1 ½ lb) smoked golden cutlets or Finnan haddock, fresh or defrosted, cut into 4
4 large eggs (size 1–2)
25 g (1 oz) butter or margarine
freshly ground black pepper
freshly grated nutmeg or chopped parsley, to garnish

1. Half-fill a large frying pan with water; add the bay leaves and the lemon slice and blades of mace, if using. Bring to the boil, add the fish and turn down to a very gentle simmer. Cover with a lid and poach for 5 minutes until the fish is cooked. Then remove the fish, pat dry if necessary with kitchen towel and place on a large serving dish. Keep warm.
2. With a slotted spoon remove the bay leaves and other flavourings from the water. Break the eggs one at a time into a cup and carefully slip into the same water. Poach gently for about 3 minutes until the whites are just firm. Do not allow more than an occasional bubble to appear in the water, or else the eggs might break up. Remove the eggs with a fish slice.
3. Dot the fish with the butter and top each with an egg. Grind a little black pepper over each and serve sprinkled with grated nutmeg or chopped parsley.

Top *Cheesy Fish Muffins*, below *Golden Fish with Poached Sunny Eggs*

Light Fish Pâté

If you can't face a cooked breakfast or if you just want a quick brunch mid-week, a pot of fish pâté is ideal to have on hand in the fridge, ready to spread on toast. This one is lighter than traditional fish pâtés too.

SERVES 4

375 g (12 oz) cooked kipper or 'hot' smoked mackerel
75 g (3 oz) low-fat spread
1–2 tablespoons natural yogurt or fromage frais
1 teaspoon grated onion (optional)
1 tablespoon chopped fresh dill or parsley (optional)
freshly ground black pepper

1. Skin the fish, carefully bone and then mash in a small bowl, or use a food processor if preferred.
2. Beat in the low-fat spread, yogurt or fromage frais, and onion and herbs, if using. Season well with pepper (no need for salt) and then spoon into a serving bowl and chill to firm up.
3. Cover to store in the fridge and eat within five days.

Omelette Arnold Bennett

Arnold Bennett was a novelist of renown at the turn of this century and at one time he was editor of a well-known women's magazine. This was one of his favourite dishes. Traditionally, smoked haddock was used in this recipe, but any other smoked fish will do.

SERVES 2

250 g (8 oz) smoked white fish fillet, fresh or defrosted
3 eggs, separated
2 tablespoons water
50 g (2 oz) mature Cheddar cheese, grated finely
a knob of butter or margarine
freshly ground black pepper
chopped fresh parsley, to garnish (optional)

1. Poach the fish in a little water for 5 minutes. Remove the skin and bones and then flake the flesh. Discard the water.
2. Beat the egg yolks with the water and three-quarters of the cheese; then season with pepper (no salt is necessary). Whisk the egg whites until they form stiff peaks and then carefully fold into the yolks, together with the fish.

3. Heat the butter or margarine in a medium-size omelette pan until it stops foaming. Pour in the mixture and cook gently until the base sets and is pale brown.
4. Meanwhile, preheat the grill and sprinkle the remaining cheese on top of the omelette as it cooks. Brown the omelette under the grill for a minute or two and serve straight away, before it starts to sink. Sprinkle with a little parsley, if liked.

Devilled Fish and Mushroom Parcels

These are good for preparing and placing in an automatic oven overnight. In warm weather use frozen fish fillets, so that they will be fresher by the time the oven switches itself on. Alternatively, prepare them the night before and store in the fridge; then get up earlier to pop them in to cook!

SERVES 4

4 white fish fillets, fresh or defrosted, each weighing about 175 g (6 oz), skinned
1 tablespoon sunflower oil
175 g (6 oz) button mushrooms, sliced
50 g (2 oz) softened butter
2 teaspoons coarse-grain mustard or mild mustard relish
a few drops of Worcestershire sauce (optional)
salt and freshly ground black pepper

1. Preheat the oven to Gas Mark 5/190°C/375°F.
2. Tear off four pieces of foil large enough to enclose the fish. Brush lightly with the oil and then place a fillet in the middle of each piece. Top with the sliced mushrooms and season.
3. Beat the butter with the mustard and add the Worcestershire sauce, if you want the sauce to be a bit spicier. Alternatively, add Worcestershire sauce separately for the adult portions. Dab the butter all over the fish and mushrooms.
4. Fold up the foil, leaving enough room to allow for steam and juices, then seal well around the edges. Place on a baking sheet and, when ready, bake for 25–30 minutes, or until firm. Serve the parcels in their foil on warmed plates and accompany with warm crusty rolls for the family to dip into the tasty juices.

Creamy Kedgeree

Kedgeree can be such a dull and dry dish, but stirring a raw beaten egg into the hot rice and fish transforms it, making it much more delicious.

SERVES 4

250 g (8 oz) long grain rice, e.g. basmati or brown rice
500 g (1 lb) smoked haddock or cod, fresh or defrosted
25 g (1 oz) butter or margarine
3 large eggs (size 1–2)
a pinch of Cayenne pepper or a few drops of hot pepper sauce
a little creamy milk
2 spring onions, chopped (optional)
salt and freshly ground black pepper
chopped fresh parsley, to garnish

1. Boil the rice in plenty of lightly salted boiling water until just tender. This will be 12 minutes for white rice and 30–40 minutes for brown rice; check your packet for full instructions. Rinse the rice with hot water and place in a large warmed serving dish.
2. At the same time, poach or grill the fish until just cooked. Remove the skin and bones and flake the flesh. Stir this into the rice, along with the butter or margarine.
3. Meanwhile, hard-boil two of the eggs and shell them. Then either chop or quarter them.
4. Beat the other egg with the Cayenne or the pepper sauce and a couple of tablespoons of the milk. Stir this into the rice along with the onions, if using. If the mixture looks too dry, add a little more milk. Check for seasoning and serve straight away, with the hard-boiled eggs and parsley sprinkled on top.

USING FROZEN FISH

For the best texture, thaw frozen fish slowly overnight in the fridge, or cook it straight from frozen, if it is not too thick.

Jugged Kippers with Lemon Butter

This is an old-fashioned and very simple way of 'cooking' kippers without using the oven or grill, and it contains any smells.

SERVES 4

4 pairs of kippers, fresh or defrosted, each weighing about 250 g (8 oz), or 8 kipper fillets, fresh or defrosted

FOR THE BUTTER:
125 g (4 oz) softened butter
grated rind of ½ lemon
1 lemon, quartered, to garnish

1. Cut the heads from the kippers and place the kippers in a large bowl or, if you have one, a tall jug. Completely cover them with boiling water and leave to stand for about 7 minutes. If your bowl or jug isn't big enough, do this in two batches. Remove the fish and pat dry with kitchen towel. Keep warm in a low oven.
2. Meanwhile, cream the butter and lemon rind together. Then dab this over the prepared kippers and serve immediately, garnished with a lemon quarter each. Brown bread and butter and simple grilled tomatoes make good accompaniments.

Herring Fingers with Crispy Bacon

These herring in oatmeal are a more appealing version of the Scottish fish dish, which children should find tasty and easier to eat.

SERVES 4

4 herring fillets
flour, to coat
1 large egg (size 2), beaten
50 g (2 oz) medium oatmeal
2 tablespoons sunflower oil
8 rashers of streaky bacon, de-rinded
1 lemon or orange, quartered, to garnish

1. Cut the herring fillets into fingers about 2.5 cm (1 inch) wide. Dip the fingers first in the flour and then in the beaten egg; lastly coat well in the oatmeal.
2. Heat the oil and fry the bacon until crisp; then drain on kitchen towel and keep warm.
3. Fry the herring strips in the pan fat, turning carefully so that they don't break up. Cook for about 5 minutes in total; then remove and drain on kitchen towel. Serve hot with the bacon and garnish each with a lemon or orange quarter.

WEEKEND FISH CAKES

Nearly everyone loves fish cakes, especially home-made ones!

MAKES 8 LARGE OR 12 MEDIUM-SIZE CAKES

about 500 g (1 lb) white fish fillets, fresh or defrosted, or 375 g (12 oz) cooked and flaked white fish, e.g. cod, haddock, coley, whiting or hake
1 small onion, chopped
25 g (1 oz) butter
750 g (1 ½ lb) potatoes, boiled and mashed, e.g. Maris Piper, Edwards or Romano
3 tablespoons chopped fresh parsley or 1 teaspoon dried mixed herbs
freshly ground nutmeg, to taste
salt and freshly ground black pepper
FOR THE COATING:
125 g (4 oz) dried natural breadcrumbs
50 g (2 oz) chopped nuts, e.g. dry-roasted peanuts, almonds, hazelnuts or chopped mixed nuts
2 eggs, beaten
oil, for frying

1. If using raw fish, cook the fillets by either poaching, grilling or baking until firm and white. Let them cool and then skin and flake the flesh, but not too finely, checking well for any bones.
2. Meanwhile, gently fry the onion in the butter for about 5 minutes and mix into the mashed potatoes. Then add the fish together with the herbs, nutmeg and plenty of seasoning. Put the mixture into a bowl; cool and chill until firm.
3. When ready to cook, divide the mixture into 8 for large fish cakes or 12 for slightly smaller ones. Shape into fairly flat rounds. Mix the crumbs and nuts together and dip the cakes first into the beaten egg and then into the crumbs, making sure they are well coated. Rest on a large plate whilst you finish the batch.
4. For the best results, and a nice crispy coating, deep-fry the fish cakes. Heat the oil to a temperature of 185°C/360°F, or until it is hot enough to brown a cube of day-old bread in under a minute. Then fry the cakes for 3–4 minutes. Otherwise, shallow-fry the cakes for about 3 minutes on each side.
5. A tangy sauce, such as home-made tomato or chutney, brown sauce or even ketchup, makes a delicious accompaniment.

Note: If you wish to freeze the fish cakes, fry for about a minute only just to seal the outside. Then drain, cool and wrap individually in freezer film. Re-heat from frozen in an oven, at Gas Mark 5/190°C/375°F. Use within six weeks.

Potted Prawns

These are ideal for preparing ahead; just turn them out of their moulds and serve with hot wholemeal toast.

SERVES 4

250 g (8 oz) peeled prawns, fresh or defrosted
½ teaspoon ground mace
a good pinch of ground ginger
a good pinch of Cayenne pepper
125 g (4 oz) unsalted butter
salt and freshly ground black pepper
lemon quarters, to garnish

1. Finely chop half the prawns and mix with the remaining whole ones. Add the spices and a little seasoning and mix in well.
2. Melt the butter and pour about three-quarters of it onto the prawns, stirring to mix.
3. Spoon the prawn mixture into four ramekins or tea cups and immediately pour over the rest of the melted butter.
4. Chill until set. Turn out onto small plates, accompanied by toast and garnished with the lemon quarters.

CHOOSING FISH

In most recipes, the fish is interchangeable according to your taste, the season and your budget. Coley is an excellent substitute for more pricey cod or haddock, and its pinky-grey colour turns to creamy-white when cooked. Mackerel can be substituted for herring, and most flat fish are interchangeable.

PICNICS, BARBECUES AND PACKED LUNCHES

If you are eating outdoors or on the move, fish really is versatile – hot or cold; whole or flaked; in soups, salads and even sandwiches. By including fish you also ensure that a picnic or packed lunch is a complete and nourishing meal in itself.

COD AND CORN CHOWDER

This is a tasty and filling main-meal soup: ideal for flasks. Ask your fishmonger to prepare the fish for you.

SERVES 4

600 ml (1 pint) milk
600 ml (1 pint) water
25 g (1 oz) butter
1 onion, chopped
250 g (8 oz) potatoes, chopped
a pinch of saffron strands or ½ teaspoon turmeric
500 g (1 lb) cod fillet or other white fish, fresh or defrosted, skinned and diced
2 slices of lean ham, cut in thin shreds
200 g (7 oz) can of sweetcorn kernels, drained
a little freshly grated nutmeg, to taste
salt and freshly ground black pepper
1 tablespoon chopped fresh parsley, to garnish

1. Heat the milk, water and butter in a saucepan; then add the onion and potato. Soak the saffron strands for a few minutes in a little warm water and add, if using. Otherwise, add the turmeric. Simmer the mixture for about 10 minutes, until softened.
2. Add the diced fish to the pan, together with the ham and corn, and simmer for another 10 minutes.
3. Check the seasoning and add the nutmeg. Stir in the parsley and either serve in bowls or pour piping hot into warmed vacuum flasks.

Top *Cod and Corn Chowder*, below *Seafish Quiche*

Seafish Quiche

Delicious warm, this flan is also excellent chilled for a picnic.

SERVES 4

FOR THE PASTRY:
250 g (8 oz) plain flour or 125 g (4 oz) each plain and wholemeal flours
125 g (4 oz) butter or margarine
a good pinch of dried mixed herbs
cold water

FOR THE FILLING:
1 small onion, sliced
1 garlic clove, crushed
25 g (1 oz) butter
2 eggs, beaten
TABASCO
300 ml (½ pint) single cream or milk
250 g (8 oz) cooked smoked haddock fillets, skinned and diced
125 g (4 oz) peeled prawns, fresh or defrosted (optional)
75 g (3 oz) Gruyère or Cheddar cheese, grated
a good pinch of ground mace or nutmeg
salt and freshly ground black pepper

1. Sift the flour or flours into a bowl. Rub in the fat and stir in the herbs; then mix to a firm dough with just enough cold water to bind.
2. Roll out and line a 23 cm (9-inch) flan dish, and lightly prick the base. Chill this for 30 minutes. Preheat the oven to Gas Mark 6/200°C/400°F.
3. Line the pastry case with foil or greaseproof paper and baking beans. Bake blind for 20 minutes, removing the beans and foil for the last 5 minutes.
4. Meanwhile, lightly sauté the onion and garlic in the butter for 5 minutes. Let them cool slightly before placing in the flan case base.
5. Mix the eggs with the cream or milk, season well and add the nutmeg or mace.
6. Scatter the diced fish and shellfish onto the onion mixture. Sprinkle the cheese over this and slowly pour on the egg and milk mixture.
7. Return to the oven at Gas Mark 4/180°C/350°F for about 35–40 minutes until risen, golden and firm. Allow to cool slightly and serve either warm or chilled.

Tomato and Fish Soup

This almost has a sunny Mediterranean feel to it – great for days when the weather is not as bright as it should be.

SERVES 4–6

2 tablespoons sunflower oil
1 onion, chopped
1 garlic clove, crushed
1 small red or green pepper, cored and chopped
400 g (14 oz) can of peeled tomatoes
1.2 litres (2 pints) fish, vegetable or chicken stock, or water
1–2 tablespoons Worcestershire sauce
375 g (12 oz) white fish fillets, fresh or defrosted, skinned and cut into chunks, e.g. cod, haddock or coley
50 g (2 oz) quick cook macaroni
½ teaspoon dried marjoram or oregano
salt and freshly ground black pepper
chopped fresh parsley, to garnish

1. Heat the oil in a large saucepan and add the onion, garlic and pepper. Fry gently for about 5 minutes, stirring occasionally, until softened.
2. Add the tomatoes, stock, sauce, fish, macaroni, marjoram or oregano and season well. Bring to the boil and simmer, covered, for 15 minutes, stirring occasionally.
3. Serve the soup in bowls sprinkled with parsley, or pour it into flasks for picnics and packed lunches. As it is a nourishing soup, it only needs a crusty wholemeal roll to complete it.

Mixed Fish Kebabs

Sometimes, fish can be a little tricky to 'kebab' unless the flesh is firm. I have found that one tasty solution is to wrap the fish chunks in thin slices of bacon. This is also a good way of 'stretching' the fish further, leaving little waste.

SERVES 4

750 g (1 ½ lb) mixed filleted fish, fresh or defrosted, skinned, e.g. haddock, coley and herring
3 tablespoons olive or sunflower oil
juice of 1 lemon
½ teaspoon mixed dried herbs or thyme
2 teaspoons finely chopped spring onion (optional)
about 12 thin rashers of streaky bacon, de-rinded
1 large onion, quartered
fresh or dried bay leaves
salt and freshly ground black pepper

1. Cut the fish into chunks about 4 cm (1 ½ inches) square. Mix these with the oil, lemon juice, herbs, spring onion and seasoning. Leave them to marinate for 30 minutes.
2. Meanwhile, cut the bacon in half to make about 24 pieces.
3. Wrap a chunk of fish at a time in the small rashers; smaller pieces of fish can be combined.
4. Separate the onion quarters into segments of the same size as the fish rolls, cutting smaller if necessary.
5. Thread the fish onto four skewers, alternating with the onion pieces and an occasional bay leaf.
6. Grill the kebabs over glowing embers for about 7 minutes on each side, or for 5 minutes on each side under a preheated grill. Baste with more oil or any leftover marinade, if you like, during cooking. These are delicious removed from the skewers and served in halved pitta breads.

Top *Soy Herring with Barbecue Sauce*, below *Mixed Fish Kebabs*

Soy Herring with Barbecue Sauce

Herring are ideal for barbecuing because they are naturally oily and need little basting. To make them easier to turn, either place in a barbecue fish holder or wrap in clean chicken wire.

SERVES 4

4 herring, preferably filleted
soy sauce, to coat
FOR THE SAUCE:
1 tablespoon cornflour
2 tablespoons water
150 ml (¼ pint) hot fish or chicken stock
4 tablespoons tomato ketchup
1–2 tablespoons Worcestershire sauce
2 tablespoons red wine or cider vinegar
2 tablespoons brown sugar
2 drops of hot pepper sauce (optional)
2 tablespoons tomato purée

1. Slash the herring twice on each side and sprinkle them lightly with the soy sauce. Rub this well in, especially into the slashes.
2. To make the sauce: blend the cornflour to a paste with the water. Place all the other ingredients in a saucepan and bring to the boil. Gradually stir in the blended cornflour and heat until the sauce is smooth and thickened. Simmer for 2 minutes and keep warm until required.
3. Grill the herring on the barbecue or under the grill, for about 5 minutes on each side.
4. Serve the herring hot, with the sauce spooned over. Grilled pitta bread and a green salad make good accompaniments.

Fish Steaks Barbecued in Foil

Prepare these before you get the barbecue ready. The foil will stop them from drying out, and they can be kept on the side of the barbecue after cooking – for up to 30 minutes, if necessary.

SERVES 4

4 white fish steaks, fresh or defrosted, each weighing about 175 g (6 oz), e.g. cod, haddock or conger eel
1 small leek, shredded finely
1 carrot, sliced finely
125 g (4 oz) button mushrooms, sliced thinly
25 g (1 oz) butter or margarine, plus extra for greasing
4 tablespoons single cream or dry sherry, or a mixture (optional)
salt and freshly ground black pepper

1. Tear off four pieces of foil, about 23 cm (9 inches) square. Grease them and then lay them on a large baking sheet – this may have to be done in relays.
2. Put a steak on each foil piece, season, and place the vegetables on top. Dot each one with the butter, spoon over the cream or sherry, and season again. Wrap up each steak well, keeping the joins on top.
3. Place the parcels on the barbecue and cook for 15 minutes over glowing embers until done, or bake at Gas Mark 5/190°C/375°F for 20 minutes. Serve the fish in their parcels, unwrapped.

Mustard Mackerel with Apple Sauce

Although gooseberry sauce is traditional with mackerel, fresh gooseberries are not always available and canned ones are too sweet. I use cooking apples instead, which are much more freely available, and the resulting sharp sweetness is just as complementary.

SERVES 4

4 mackerel each weighing about 375 g (12 oz), cleaned
4 teaspoons coarse-grain or French mustard
juice of 1 lemon

FOR THE SAUCE:
2 Bramley cooking apples, peeled and chopped
1–2 tablespoons water
25 g (1 oz) butter or margarine
a pinch of dill weed
salt and freshly ground black pepper

1. Cut the heads off the mackerel if you like; slash the bodies twice on each side.
2. Mix the mustard and lemon juice together and spoon over the mackerel, rubbing well in. Leave the fish to marinate for about 30 minutes.
3. Meanwhile, make the sauce: simmer the apples with the water, butter or margarine, dill weed and seasoning for about 10 minutes, until soft and pulpy. Beat with a spoon if you want a smooth sauce, otherwise leave it slightly chunky.
4. Grill the mackerel for about 5 minutes on each side, until cooked. This can be done over a barbecue – in which case cook in a fish holder or wrap in clean chicken wire.
5. Serve the fish hot, with the sauce.

Crab-stuffed Eggs

This is a pretty starter for a patio meal.

SERVES 4–6

6 large eggs (size 1), hard-boiled and halved
125 g (4 oz) crab meat, preferably white, fresh or defrosted
1 tablespoon mayonnaise
2 teaspoons tomato relish (optional)
a few drops of hot pepper sauce (optional)
1 tablespoon fresh chives or spring onion tops, chopped finely
salt and freshly ground black pepper
a pack of mixed salad leaves, including radicchio, to serve (optional)

1. Spoon out the egg yolks and put them into a large bowl, keeping the egg whites on one side. Mash the yolks with a fork and mix with the crab meat, mayonnaise and relish. Add the pepper sauce for the adult portions and mix well in.
2. Check the seasoning and spoon the mixture back into the egg whites, piling it up. Sprinkle the chives or the spring onion tops over the eggs. Arrange salad leaves on a plate, if you like, and place the eggs on top. Chill until required.

Mackerel and Coleslaw Pitta Pockets

These are simple to make, easy to eat and very tasty.

MAKES 4

1 'hot' smoked mackerel fillet, fresh or defrosted, weighing about 175 g (6 oz)
250 g (8 oz) carton of coleslaw
2 whole pitta breads, halved, or 4 mini pittas
2 tomatoes, sliced
lettuce, shredded, to serve

1. Skin and flake the mackerel; then mix it with the coleslaw.
2. Open up the pittas, taking care not to split the sides. Fill them with the tomato slices, shredded lettuce and the mackerel and coleslaw. Wrap them in cling film, until ready to use.

Tuna Salad Sandwiches

MAKES 4 ROUNDS

200 g (7 oz) can of tuna fish in oil or brine, drained
1 egg, hard-boiled and chopped
2 teaspoons tomato relish
1 spring onion, chopped
1 stick of celery, sliced finely
2–3 tablespoons mayonnaise
2 teaspoons fresh lemon juice
8 slices of wholemeal bread, buttered if wished
4 lettuce leaves
salt and freshly ground black pepper

1. Flake the fish and put it into a mixing bowl with the egg, relish, onion, celery, mayonnaise and lemon juice. Season and mix well.
2. Divide the mixture between four of the bread slices, top with a lettuce leaf and finish with a final slice of bread each. Cut them in half and wrap in cling film, until needed.

Note: these can be made the night before, but do not freeze them.

Treasure Chests

The Victorians called these deep rolls filled with salad 'portable salads'. I've adapted the idea for my children, using brown loaf-shaped rolls filled with a cooked and chilled smoked fish salad.

MAKES 4

4 brown loaf-shaped rolls or other deep bread rolls
soft margarine or low-fat spread, for spreading
125 g (4 oz) cooked, skinned and flaked smoked fish fillets, e.g. haddock, cod or kipper
about 175 g (6 oz) mixed crisp salad vegetables, e.g. crisp lettuce, cucumber, etc.
1 tablespoon mayonnaise or salad cream
1 tablespoon natural yogurt
a good pinch of dried dill weed
salt and freshly ground black pepper

1. Cut the tops off the rolls and hollow out, discarding the insides. Spread the rolls with the margarine or low-fat spread.
2. Mix the fish, salad vegetables, mayonnaise or salad cream, yogurt and dill weed in a bowl and season well.
3. Spoon the mixture into the centre of the rolls and replace the tops. Wrap them in cling film until required.

Note: these can be made the night before, but do not freeze them.

WHITE FISH AND TOMATO BAPS

We are used to eating cold canned fish and yet, surprisingly, we hesitate about eating cold, cooked white fish. It really is delicious – try it!

MAKES 4 BAPS

2 frozen white fish steaks each weighing 100 g (3½ oz), e.g. cod, haddock or coley
juice of ½ lemon
sunflower oil, for brushing
2 medium-size tomatoes, quartered, de-seeded and sliced
4 teaspoons mayonnaise or salad cream
a few sprigs of watercress
4 wholemeal baps, split and buttered lightly
salt and freshly ground black pepper

1. Preheat the grill. Brush the fish steaks with the lemon juice and oil and season lightly. Grill the fish for about 4 minutes on each side and cool; then flake the flesh.
2. Mix the fish with the tomatoes, mayonnaise or salad cream and watercress. Pile the mixture into the four baps. Wrap in cling film and chill until required.

Note: these can be made the night before, but do not freeze them.

SARDINE, CUCUMBER AND DILL IN RYE

Try this updated version of a traditional family favourite.

MAKES 4 ROUNDS

200 g (7 oz) can of sardines in oil, drained
juice of ½ lemon
8 slices of rye bread, buttered lightly
7.5 cm (3-inch) piece of cucumber, sliced thinly
1 tablespoon chopped fresh dill weed or 1 teaspoon dried dill weed
salt and freshly ground black pepper

1. Flake the sardines, season well and mix with the lemon juice.
2. Divide the fish between four of the slices of rye bread and layer with the cucumber. Sprinkle over the dill weed, and sandwich each with a final slice of bread. Wrap them in cling film, until ready to use.

Note: these can be made the night before, but do not freeze them.

Tasty Turnovers

Ask your fishmonger to prepare the fish for you.

SERVES 4

250 g (8 oz) shortcrust pastry (see p. 22)
2 leeks, sliced
25 g (1 oz) butter or 2 tablespoons sunflower oil
1 teaspoon mild curry powder
125 g (4 oz) button mushrooms, sliced thinly
375 g (12 oz) white fish fillets, fresh or defrosted, e.g. haddock, coley or cod, or a half-and-half mixture of white fish fillets and smoked fish fillets, skinned
2 tablespoons natural yogurt or single cream
a squeeze of fresh lemon juice
1 egg, beaten
salt and freshly ground black pepper

1. Roll out the pastry thinly on a lightly floured board, and cut out four squares measuring about 13 cm (5 inches), re-rolling as necessary. Put on one side. Preheat the oven to Gas Mark 6/200°C/400°F.
2. Sauté the leeks in the butter or oil for 5 minutes, until softened. Add the curry powder and cook for another minute. Stir in the mushrooms and then cook for 2 more minutes.
3. Cut the fish into chunks and add to the pan with some seasoning. Cover and cook for 5 minutes, stirring carefully once or twice. Stir in the yogurt or cream and a squeeze of lemon juice.
4. Allow the mixture to cool and then divide it between the four squares. Brush the edges of the pastry squares with beaten egg and fold each square in half diagonally. Seal and crimp the edges and glaze the tops well.
5. Bake for 20–25 minutes, until they are golden brown. Remove and cool.

Top *Tasty Turnovers*, below *Rollmop and Potato Salad*

Rollmop and Potato Salad

A Scandinavian-style salad, using ready-prepared rollmop herring. Try accompanying it with sliced cooked beetroot.

SERVES 4

6 rollmop herring, drained
250 g (8 oz) new potatoes, scrubbed and cooked
1 small onion, sliced thinly
1 green dessert apple, cored and sliced thinly
150 g carton of soured cream or natural yogurt, or a half-and-half mixture
a squeeze of lemon juice (optional)
2 tablespoons chopped fresh parsley
salt and freshly ground black pepper
sprigs of watercress, to garnish

1. Cut the herring in half, checking for any bones, and removing any tail fins.
2. Slice the potatoes if they are large. Mix carefully in a bowl with the onion, apple, soured cream or natural yogurt, lemon juice, if liked, and parsley. Check the seasoning.
3. Chill before serving, garnished with the watercress leaves, or spoon it into tubs for taking on picnics and packed lunches.

Prawn and Cucumber Dip

Pack this up in a tub with savoury biscuits and slices of pitta bread.

SERVES 4

200 g packet of low-fat soft cheese
3 tablespoons natural yogurt
1 tablespoon chopped fresh chives or spring onion tops
1 tablespoon chopped fresh parsley
7.5 cm (3-inch) piece of cucumber, grated
125 g (4 oz) peeled prawns, fresh or defrosted, chopped
a few drops of hot pepper sauce or a good pinch of Cayenne pepper (optional)
salt and freshly ground black pepper

1. Blend the soft cheese and yogurt together and mix in the other ingredients.
2. Check the seasoning, spoon into a plastic tub and chill until required. Serve within 8 hours, with fresh vegetable sticks.

Note: do not use this for packed lunches in warm weather, unless it is chilled and then packed in a cool box or insulated bag.

Fish, Pea and Pasta Salad

This tasty main-meal salad is ideal for packed lunches and picnics: spoon it into tubs to take with you.

SERVES 4

250 g (8 oz) pasta or macaroni
2 tablespoons french dressing
125 g (4 oz) frozen peas, cooked
125 g (4 oz) sweetcorn, cooked if frozen
500 g (1 lb) white or smoked fish fillets, fresh or defrosted, cooked, skinned and flaked
2 dill pickle cucumbers, chopped
3 tablespoons mayonnaise or salad cream
2 tablespoons single cream or natural yogurt
2 spring onions, chopped
2 tablespoons chopped fresh parsley
salt and freshly ground black pepper

1. Cook the pasta according to packet instructions. Drain, rinse and then toss in the dressing to cool.
2. When the pasta is cold, mix it with the peas, corn, flaked fish and cucumber and then season to taste.
3. Mix together the mayonnaise or salad cream, cream or yogurt, onions and parsley, and stir this into the salad.

Highland Herring Soup

SERVES 4

25 g (1 oz) butter or margarine
1 onion, chopped
1 medium-size leek, sliced
1 carrot, peeled and chopped
400 g (14 oz) can of chopped tomatoes
900 ml (1 ½ pints) water
1–2 tablespoons wine vinegar
2 tablespoons pearl barley
3 herring fillets, sliced
salt and freshly ground black pepper

1. Melt the butter in a large saucepan and add the onion, leek and carrot. Sauté for 5 minutes, until softened.
2. Add the tomatoes, 600 ml (1 pint) of the water, the vinegar and barley. Season, bring to the boil and cover; simmer gently for 25 minutes.
3. Add the rest of the water, return to the boil, and add the herring pieces. Continue to simmer for another 8–10 minutes. Check the seasoning and serve hot in bowls, or pour into warmed vacuum flasks.

High Teas, Suppers and Salads

When you want to give the family a quick, filling and nourishing meal at the end of the day, fish really does come into its own. It is versatile and easy to prepare. Canned fish is also useful because you can serve it simply on toast or mix it with other ingredients for a more filling dish.

Italian Fish and Green Bean Frittata

This is similar to a quiche without the pastry base although it is prepared like a large omelette. However, unlike an omelette it is cooked slowly and left flat. Try using other vegetables instead of beans; almost any kind are delicious cooked this way. In summer serve it with a green salad; in winter it is good with plain boiled potatoes. It can be served either hot or cold.

SERVES 4

250 g (8 oz) white or smoked fish fillets, fresh or defrosted
125 g (4 oz) green beans, topped and halved
1 small onion, sliced
6 eggs
2 tablespoons sunflower or olive oil
2 tomatoes, sliced
2 tablespoons grated parmesan cheese
salt and freshly ground black pepper

1. Grill or poach the fish, skin it and flake the flesh.
2. Cook the beans and onion in a little water for about 5 minutes, until just tender; then drain.
3. Beat the eggs well, adding seasoning. Heat the oil in a large non-stick frying pan and pour in the eggs. On the lowest heat possible, cook the eggs, without stirring, for about 5 minutes.
4. Sprinkle over the fish, beans and onion; cook for another 5 minutes.
5. Arrange the tomatoes on top, sprinkle over the cheese and continue cooking until the whole of the mixture is set. It may be necessary to grill the top if it is still a little runny.
6. Slide the frittata off onto a serving plate and serve hot. Otherwise allow it to get cold and serve cut in wedges.

Top *Italian Fish and Green Bean Frittata*, below *Smoked Fish Florentine*

SMOKED FISH FLORENTINE

We all know spinach is full of good things like iron and fibre; combined with high-protein fish and a cheese sauce, it becomes a very nutritious meal that is tasty too.

SERVES 4

500 g (1 lb) fresh spinach or 300 g (10.3 oz) packet of frozen leaf spinach, defrosted
500 g (1 lb) smoked white fish fillets, fresh or defrosted, skinned, e.g. haddock, cod or whiting
450 ml (¾ pint) milk
2 bay leaves
1 tablespoon cornflour
2 tablespoons water
75 g (3 oz) mature Cheddar cheese, grated
freshly ground black pepper

1. For fresh spinach, wash well, shake the excess water off and cook in a covered saucepan for about 6 minutes, until just wilted. Drain well and place on the base of a shallow ovenproof dish. If using frozen spinach, heat briefly in a saucepan, without extra water, for 2 minutes. Drain, squeezing out any excess water, and place in the dish.
2. Meanwhile, poach the fish in the milk, with the bay leaves and pepper, for 10 minutes. Remove the bay leaves and remove the fish with a fish slice. Place on top of the spinach.
3. Mix the cornflour with the water in a cup; stir into the milk.
4. Return the milk to the boil, stirring until it has thickened. Simmer for a minute and then mix in two-thirds of the cheese, until melted. Pour this over the fish.
5. Top with the remaining cheese and brown under a hot grill, until golden and bubbling. Serve hot as soon as possible, with pasta or potatoes, or simply brown bread and butter.

Light and Tasty Battered Fish

Fish and chips is nearly everyone's favourite meal, but more and more people now prefer a lighter batter. Here is one that is based on the very light Japanese tempura batter. For best results, both the batter and fish should be as cold as possible and the oil good and hot.

SERVES 4

125 g (4 oz) plain flour
½ teaspoon baking powder
½ teaspoon onion salt
1 chicken stock cube, crumbled
1 egg
90 ml (3 fl oz) milk
90 ml (3 fl oz) water
4 round or flat white fish fillets, fresh or defrosted, each weighing about 250 g (8 oz), skinned
oil, for deep-frying
salt and freshly ground black pepper

1. Sift the flour, baking powder and onion salt into a large bowl. Crumble in the stock cube and mix in well.
2. Make a well in the centre and add the egg. Gradually beat the egg and flour together, adding the milk and water slowly until you have a thick, smooth batter. Check the seasoning.
3. Pat the fish dry with kitchen towel, checking for any pin bones.
4. Fill a deep-fat frying pan a third full of oil and heat to a temperature of 185°C/360°F, or until a cube of day-old bread browns in 30 seconds.
5. Dip the fish in the batter, immersing completely.
6. Fry the fillets in two batches, making sure that you re-heat the oil in between. Using the wire chip basket, lower the fish carefully into the hot fat and cook for about 3 minutes, until golden brown. Remove and drain. Keep the first batch warm in a low oven, uncovered, while the second batch are cooking. Serve immediately, with chips.

Fish Fingers Danish-style

MAKES 10

1 packet of 10 fish fingers
oil, for frying
150 ml (5 fl oz) carton of soured cream
1 tablespoon sandwich spread
1 tomato, quartered, de-seeded and chopped
7.5 cm (3-inch) piece of cucumber, de-seeded and sliced
lettuce leaves, to serve
parsley sprigs, to garnish

1. Fry or grill the fish fingers according to packet instructions. For really crisp results, deep-fry in hot oil. Drain and cool.
2. Mix together the soured cream, sandwich spread and chopped tomato. Spoon it on top of the fish fingers and arrange the sliced cucumber on top.
3. Serve chilled on lettuce leaves, garnished with the parsley sprigs.

Mushroom-stuffed Fish Rolls

SERVES 4

4 plaice, dab or lemon sole fillets, fresh or defrosted, each weighing 175 g (6 oz), skinned
25 g (1 oz) butter
juice of ½ lemon
a pinch of dried mixed herbs
125 g (4 oz) button mushrooms, sliced thinly
2 spring onions, chopped
40 g (1½ oz) Cheddar cheese, grated
1 tablespoon dried natural breadcrumbs
salt and freshly ground black pepper

1. Place the fillets, skinned-side up, on a board and season lightly. Preheat the oven to Gas Mark 5/190°C/375°F.
2. Melt half the butter in a saucepan and add the lemon juice, herbs and seasoning. Add the mushrooms and onions, cover and cook over a gentle heat for 5 minutes.
3. Divide the mixture between the fillets and roll each one up. Place them, join-side down, in a shallow ovenproof dish. Dot with the remaining butter, brushing over the fish surface if possible.
4. Sprinkle over the cheese and breadcrumbs. Bake for about 15 minutes, until the tops are golden and crispy. Serve hot.

Top *Fish Fingers Danish-style*, below *Mushroom-stuffed Fish Rolls*

Fishy Dippers

I suppose these are the nearest one can get to making home-made fish fingers. For fun, serve them 'in the basket' with small pots of tomato sauce or salad cream for children to dip into.

SERVES 4

500 g (1 lb) white fish fillets, fresh or defrosted, skinned, e.g. plaice, dab, sole or haddock
1 large egg (size 1), beaten
75 g (3 oz) dried natural breadcrumbs
1 teaspoon onion salt
1 teaspoon dried mixed herbs
oil, for deep-fat frying
salt and freshly ground black pepper

1. Check the fish for pin bones and cut into fingers about 2.5 cm (1 inch) thick on the diagonal.
2. Season the beaten egg. Mix the breadcrumbs with the onion salt and the herbs. Dip the fish strips first in the egg and then into the crumbs. Set them aside on a plate, in a single layer.
3. Fill a deep-fat frying pan a third full of oil and heat to a temperature of 185°C/360°F, or until a cube of day-old bread browns in 30 seconds.
4. Deep-fry the dippers in batches, for just under 2 minutes, until golden brown and crisp. Drain on kitchen paper. For best results, allow the fat to return to temperature in between. Serve hot and allow your children to eat with their fingers.

Sweetcorn and Fish Fritters

These are very popular with children because they are easy to eat, especially with their fingers.

MAKES 12–15

125 g (4 oz) plain flour
1 teaspoon baking powder
1 teaspoon salt
1 large egg (size 2)
125 ml (4 fl oz) milk
250 g (8 oz) smoked fish fillets, fresh or defrosted, skinned and diced finely
½ x 200 g (7 oz) can of sweetcorn, drained
3–4 tablespoons sunflower oil, for frying
freshly ground black pepper

1. Sift the flour, with the baking powder and salt, into a bowl. Make a well in the centre and add the egg. Gradually mix the two together, adding milk as the mixture thickens. Season with pepper.
2. Stir in the fish and the corn.
3. Heat the oil in a large frying pan and, when it is quite hot, drop in dessertspoonfuls of batter mixture. Cook for about 2 minutes on one side; then with a palette knife flip over and cook the other side. If the fritters look as if they are overbrowning, reduce the heat. Drain and keep warm.

Note: the batter can be made in a food processor, but stir the fish and corn in by hand.

Two Fish Burgers

MAKES 8

3 thick slices of white bread, crusts removed
250 g (8 oz) white fish fillets, fresh or defrosted, skinned, e.g. coley, cod, haddock or hake
250 g (8 oz) smoked white fish fillets, fresh or defrosted, skinned, e.g. golden cutlets
1 small onion, quartered
1 teaspoon dried mixed herbs (optional)
oil, for frying
salt and freshly ground black pepper

1. Dry the bread out in a low oven for 1 hour and then process or crush with a rolling pin, until fine.
2. Process the fish with the onion until coarsely 'minced'. Do not over-process or you will end up with a purée. Season well and add the herbs, if liked.
3. Shape into 8 small and flat round patties, using wet hands if the mixture sticks.
4. Press both sides into the breadcrumbs and set aside.
5. Heat the oil in a frying pan and shallow-fry in two batches, allowing about 3 minutes for each side. Take care that the burgers do not burn. Keep the first batch warm while frying the second.
6. Serve the burgers as they are, with chips; or try serving them in burger buns or halved pitta breads with lettuce leaves, tomato slices and cucumber. They are also delicious topped with a quarter of a cheese slice each and lightly grilled until the cheese just melts.

Fish and Bean Jackets

SERVES 4

4 baking potatoes each weighing 250 g (8 oz)
a little sunflower oil
a knob of butter or margarine
225 g can of baked beans
375 g (12 oz) cooked fish fillets, flaked, e.g. white fish, smoked fish or 'hot' smoked mackerel
40 g (1 ½ oz) Cheddar cheese, grated
grated nutmeg
salt and freshly ground black pepper

1. Preheat the oven to Gas Mark 5/190°C/375°F.
2. Cut a large cross in the tops of the potatoes. Rub with oil and bake for about 1 ¼ hours, until soft.
3. Remove and, when cool enough to handle in a tea towel, cut open carefully. Scrape out the flesh into a bowl. Mash with a knob of butter or margarine and season with nutmeg, salt and pepper.
4. Mix in the beans and fish. Spoon back into the potato jackets, re-shaping them. Place on the baking sheet, sprinkle over with cheese and return to the oven for a further 10–15 minutes, until the cheese turns golden and bubbly.

Storecupboard Sardine Pizza

SERVES 4

280 g packet of bread mix
2 tablespoons sunflower oil
1 large onion, sliced
1 garlic clove, crushed (optional)
400 g (14 oz) can of chopped or peeled tomatoes
2 x 120 g can of sardines in olive oil
75 g (3 oz) Cheddar cheese, grated
a good pinch of dried oregano, marjoram or basil
salt and freshly ground black pepper

1. Make up the bread mix, but knead it for a couple of minutes only. Roll or pat out to a 25 cm (10-inch) round.
2. Place the dough on a lightly greased baking sheet and set aside for about 10 minutes, to prove. Preheat the oven to Gas Mark 7/220°C/425°F.
3. Meanwhile, heat the oil and sauté the onion and garlic for 5 minutes. Add the tomatoes and seasoning and simmer for 10 minutes.
4. Allow this to cool slightly and spoon it over the pizza base. Arrange the sardines in a wheel pattern on top, trickling over any oil. Sprinkle with the cheese, followed by the herbs.
5. Bake for 15–20 minutes, until firm and golden. Serve immediately.

Pilchard and Egg Risotto

Another good storecupboard standby that is highly nutritious.

SERVES 4

250 g (8 oz) long grain or risotto brown rice
2 tablespoons mayonnaise
3 spring onions, chopped
2 tablespoons chopped fresh parsley
1 carrot, grated
400 g can of pilchards in tomato sauce, flaked lightly
2 eggs, hard-boiled and quartered
salt and freshly ground black pepper

1. Boil the rice according to packet instructions. Drain and mix in the mayonnaise.
2. Stir in the spring onions, parsley, carrot and the pilchards with their sauce.
3. Season and spoon into an ovenproof casserole dish. Place in a moderate oven just to heat through.
4. Place the eggs on top and serve hot.

Fish Supper Soup

SERVES 4

25 g (1 oz) butter or margarine
2 tablespoons water
500 g (1 lb) jerusalem artichokes, turnips or parsnips, peeled and diced
250 g (8 oz) leeks, sliced thinly
900 ml (1 ½ pints) fish or chicken stock
400 g (14 oz) can of tomatoes
1 teaspoon dried marjoram, oregano or mixed herbs
500 g (1 lb) white fish fillets, fresh or defrosted, skinned and cut into bite-size pieces
salt and freshly ground black pepper
leek tops, shredded, to garnish (optional)

1. In a large saucepan, melt the butter with the water, add the vegetables and cook gently. Cover the pan and cook on a low heat for about 10 minutes.
2. Add the stock, tomatoes, herbs and seasoning. Bring to the boil and then simmer gently for about 20 minutes, until the vegetables are just tender.
3. Add the fish, return to a simmer and cook for 10 minutes. Serve hot, garnished with a few shreds of the green leek tops, if wished. Crusty bread or rolls are a good accompaniment.

Crab and Cottage Cheese Flan

This is a light fish flan. Ask your fishmonger to prepare the crab meat for you.

SERVES 4

FOR THE PASTRY:
250 g (8 oz) plain flour or 125 g (4 oz) each plain and wholemeal flours
125 g (4 oz) butter or margarine
cold water
FOR THE FILLING:
250 g (8 oz) crab meat, white, brown or a half-and-half mixture, fresh or defrosted
3 spring onions, chopped finely
2 tablespoons chopped fresh parsley
a few drops of hot pepper sauce or a pinch of Cayenne pepper
2 eggs plus 1 egg yolk
250 g (8 oz) carton of cottage cheese
salt and freshly ground black pepper

1. Rub the flours and the fat together until they resemble fine breadcrumbs; then mix to a firm dough with enough cold water to bind. Roll out and line a 23 cm (9-inch) flan dish, prick the base lightly and chill for 30 minutes. Preheat the oven to Gas Mark 6/200°C/ 400°F.
2. Line the pastry case with foil or greaseproof paper and baking beans. Bake blind for 20 minutes, removing the beans and foil for the last 5 minutes.
3. Mix all the filling ingredients together, season to taste, and spoon them into the flan case.
4. Return the flan to the oven at Gas Mark 4/180°C/350°F for a further 35 minutes, or until golden brown and risen. Cool slightly, and serve warm or cool.

Salad Niçoise

SERVES 4

125 g (4 oz) green beans, topped
1 small cos lettuce
1 small onion, sliced thinly
4 ripe tomatoes, sliced thinly
200 g (7 oz) can of tuna in oil or brine, drained and flaked
4 tablespoons french dressing
2 tablespoons chopped fresh parsley
4 eggs, hard-boiled and quartered
90 g can of anchovy fillets (optional)
about 16–20 pitted black olives (optional)
salt and freshly ground black pepper

1. Boil the beans for about 3 minutes until just cooked but still crisp. Drain and cool in a sieve under cold running water and set aside.
2. Tear the lettuce into bite-size pieces and put into a large bowl with the onion, tomatoes, beans and tuna. Toss in the dressing, parsley and seasoning to taste.
3. Arrange on plates or in soup bowls, topped with the egg quarters. If using anchovies, drain well and rinse in cold water. Pat dry and cut in half lengthways. Arrange on top with the olives, if liked.

Lemony Prawn Salad

SERVES 4

250–375 g (8–12 oz) peeled prawns, fresh or defrosted
rind and juice of 1 lemon
3 spring onions, chopped
3 celery sticks, sliced thinly
1 large Granny Smith apple, cored and sliced thinly
3 tablespoons mayonnaise
2 tablespoons natural yogurt
a good pinch of dried thyme or dill weed
freshly ground black pepper
lettuce leaves, to serve
tomato quarters, to garnish

1. Sprinkle the prawns with half the lemon juice and season lightly with black pepper. Mix with the onions, celery and apple.
2. Mix the mayonnaise with the yogurt, lemon rind, remaining juice and herbs. Mix this into the prawns and vegetables or serve separately, if wished.
3. Arrange the salad on plates on the lettuce leaves, garnished with the tomato quarters. Serve with brown bread and butter.

Top *Salad Niçoise*, below *Lemony Prawn Salad*

Mackerel Macaroni Salad

'Hot' smoked mackerel is an excellent fish to use for salads because it is quickly skinned and flaked, with the minimum of waste.

SERVES 4

250 g (8 oz) quick cook macaroni
3 tablespoons french dressing
2 tablespoons chopped fresh parsley
3 spring onions, chopped
1 carrot, grated
2 tomatoes, quartered, de-seeded and sliced
50 g (2 oz) black olives (optional)
250 g (8 oz) 'hot' smoked mackerel fillets, skinned and flaked
salt and freshly ground black pepper

1. Boil the macaroni according to packet instructions. Drain, rinse and then toss in the french dressing. Allow to cool.
2. Mix in the parsley, onion, carrot, tomatoes and olives, if using.
3. Mix in the fish and check the seasoning. Chill before serving.

Pan-fried Fish with Peanut and Lemon Sauce

This really is a protein-packed meal; it is just right for the family to come home to, and a nice change from the usual fried fish.

SERVES 4

4 white fish fillets, fresh or defrosted, each weighing about 175–250 g (6–8 oz), skinned
5 tablespoons wholemeal flour
1 teaspoon dried mixed herbs
40 g (1 ½ oz) butter
2 tablespoons sunflower oil
50 g (2 oz) shelled unsalted peanuts
juice of 1 lemon
salt and freshly ground black pepper

1. Toss the fish with the flour, herbs and seasoning in a large polythene food bag. Remove and shake off the excess flour.
2. Heat half the butter and oil in a large frying pan. Fry the fish on a medium heat for 5 minutes on each side, making sure that the butter does not burn.
3. Remove the fish and drain on kitchen towel. Add the peanuts to the pan with the remaining butter and oil and fry for about a minute, stirring.
4. Pour in the lemon juice, swirl around, and spoon the lemony nuts over the fish. Serve hot.

Fish and Prawn Macaroni Cheese

A family favourite for slightly more special occasions, like a weekend high tea. I have found that children who are a little hesitant about eating fish enjoy the flavour and texture of prawns.

SERVES 4–6

250 g (8 oz) macaroni or pasta shapes
1 onion, chopped
500 g (1 lb) white fish fillets, fresh or defrosted, skinned and cubed, e.g. cod, whiting, pollack or ling
450 ml (3/4 pint) milk
2 bay leaves
1/2 teaspoon grated nutmeg or mace
125–175 g (4–6 oz) peeled prawns, fresh or defrosted
1 tablespoon cornflour
2 tablespoons water
125 g (4 oz) grated Cheddar cheese
2 tablespoons chopped fresh parsley
3 tablespoons dried natural breadcrumbs
1 tablespoon parmesan cheese
salt and freshly ground black pepper

1. Boil the macaroni or pasta shapes according to packet instructions, together with the onion; then drain and rinse.
2. Meanwhile, poach the fish in the milk with the bay leaves, nutmeg or mace and seasoning, for 10 minutes. Add the prawns a minute or two before the end.
3. Blend the cornflour with the water and stir into the fish mixture. Bring slowly to the boil, stirring until smooth and thickened. Season, remove from the heat, and stir in the cheese and parsley. Remove the bay leaf.
4. When the cheese has melted, mix in the pasta and spoon into a large heatproof dish. Sprinkle over the breadcrumbs and parmesan and place under a preheated grill to brown. Serve hot with peas, beans or lightly cooked cabbage.

Tuna, Noodle and Broccoli Crunchy Supper

Fish, broccoli and pasta are a lovely combination; together they make a tasty and colourful meal.

SERVES 4

1 onion, chopped
2 large carrots, sliced
40 g (1 ½ oz) butter or margarine
250 g (8 oz) broccoli, trimmed and cut into florets
600 ml (1 pint) milk
198 g (7 oz) can of tuna in oil or brine, drained and flaked
250 g (8 oz) flat noodles (tagliatelle), cooked
2 tablespoons flour
1 teaspoon dried mixed herbs
a good pinch of nutmeg
75 g (3 oz) Cheddar cheese, grated
a small packet of crisps, crushed
salt and freshly ground black pepper

1. Cook the onion and carrot in half the butter for about 5 minutes until softened and then add the broccoli and milk. Bring slowly to the boil, cover and simmer for a further 5 minutes until the florets are just cooked. Drain, reserving the liquid, and mix the vegetables with the tuna. Stir this into the cooked pasta and spoon into a large *gratin*-type dish.
2. Melt the remaining butter or margarine, stir in the flour and then gradually stir in the reserved liquid. Bring to the boil, stirring until the sauce is smooth and thickened. Add the herbs and nutmeg, check for seasoning, and stir in the cheese until melted.
3. Pour the sauce over the noodles, stirring lightly to incorporate, and then sprinkle the crushed crisps over the top. Keep warm in a low oven until ready to serve.

SMOKED FISH AND CHEESE SOUFFLÉ

A soufflé really isn't difficult to make, in fact it can be made a couple of hours or so in advance and kept in the fridge before baking. But remember not to open the oven door whilst cooking. Once baked it should be slightly soft in the centre and a little wobbly; then it must be served immediately, as it will sink within a minute or two.

SERVES 4

oil, for greasing
2 tablespoons dried natural breadcrumbs
375 g (12 oz) smoked fish fillets, fresh or defrosted, skinned
300 ml (½ pint) milk
a good pinch of dried thyme
40 g (1½ oz) butter or margarine
1 small onion, chopped
50 g (2 oz) flour
½ teaspoon mustard powder
125 g (4 oz) mature Cheddar cheese, grated
4 eggs, separated
salt and freshly ground black pepper

1. Preheat the oven to Gas Mark 4/180°C/350°F.
2. Grease a medium-size soufflé dish (about 1.5-litre (3-pint) capacity), and dust the sides with the dried breadcrumbs. Shake out the excess.
3. Poach the fish in the milk with the thyme for 5 minutes, and then drain the milk and reserve. Flake the fish quite finely.
4. In a large saucepan, melt the butter or margarine and gently fry the onion for about 5 minutes, until softened. Stir in the flour and mustard and cook for a minute.
5. Gradually blend in the milk, stirring until thickened: the mixture will be quite thick. Bubble for a minute and remove from the heat. Stir in most of the cheese, reserving a tablespoonful for the top.
6. Beat in the egg yolks and then stir in the fish. Check the seasoning.
7. In a large, spotlessly clean bowl, whisk the egg whites with a pinch of salt until they form stiff peaks, but are not too dry.
8. Beat a tablespoonful of the egg white into the fish mixture to loosen it; then carefully fold in the remainder with a large metal spoon. Take care not to over-mix, it doesn't matter if there are still a few pockets of foam.
9. Gently spoon into the soufflé dish, sprinkle over the reserved cheese, and place in the centre of the oven. Bake for about 35–40 minutes, until risen and golden brown. Serve and eat immediately.

Fish Charlotte

This dish is perfect for those times – on cold days – when a filling high tea would be most welcome. It is also ideal for those who dislike making pastry, because the topping is made from bread.

SERVES 4

50 g (2 oz) butter or margarine
1 onion, sliced
3 celery sticks, sliced thinly
3 carrots, sliced thinly
125 g (4 oz) button mushrooms, halved
400 g (14 oz) can of peeled or chopped tomatoes
1 teaspoon dried mixed herbs
150 ml (¼ pint) water
500 g (1 lb) white fish fillets, fresh or defrosted, skinned and cut into chunks
3–4 slices of wholemeal bread, crusts removed
salt and freshly ground black pepper

1. Preheat the oven to Gas Mark 5/190°C/375°F.
2. Melt half the butter or margarine in a saucepan and gently fry the onion, celery and carrots for about 10 minutes.
3. Add the mushrooms, tomatoes, herbs and water. Season, bring to the boil and simmer for 5 minutes.
4. Put the fish into a medium-size baking or soufflé dish and pour over the vegetable mixture. Stir briefly to incorporate.
5. Spread the slices of bread with the remaining butter or margarine, cut in half and arrange on top, buttered-side up.
6. Bake for about 30 minutes, until the bread is golden and crispy. Serve hot with green vegetables.

Smoked Mackerel Toasties

For children you may have to omit the mustard and reduce the amount of horseradish.

MAKES 4

8 slices of high-fibre white or wheatmeal bread
butter or margarine, to spread, if necessary
English or coarse grain mustard, to spread (optional)
500 g (1 lb) 'hot' smoked mackerel fillets, skinned and flaked
1 tablespoon creamed horseradish
1 celery stick, sliced thinly
tomato quarters, to serve

1. If you have a sandwich toaster, lightly spread one side of the bread with butter or margarine. If using a grill, there is no need to do this.
2. Spread four slices of bread with mustard, to taste, if wished.
3. Mix the fish, horseradish and celery together, divide between the four slices and top with the four remaining slices. Press firmly together and toast or grill until golden and crispy.
4. Serve hot, with tomato quarters and a salad.

Note: for sandwich toasters, the buttered side of the bread must be kept on the outside.

Herring Roes on Toast

In the early spring, when herring are plump with roes, you get almost two meals for the price of one! Don't throw away the roes, they make a very quick and tasty snack. If you don't want to eat them immediately, simply wrap and freeze for later. Both the hard and soft roes are suitable, and some fishmongers sell them separately.

SERVES 4

250 g (8 oz) hard or soft herring roes
3 tablespoons wholemeal flour
½ teaspoon dry mustard powder (optional)
4 slices of bread
50 g (2 oz) butter
chopped fresh parsley, to garnish
1 lemon, cut into 4, to garnish
2 tomatoes, sliced, to garnish

1. Toss the roes in the flour and mustard, if using. Shake off any excess.
2. Toast the bread and spread lightly with some of the butter.
3. Fry the roes in the remaining butter, for about 4 minutes on each side. Divide between the four slices of toast.
4. Sprinkle with parsley and serve immediately, garnished with the lemon wedges and the tomato slices.

Main Meals

There are many popular, main-meal dishes that can use fish, including a number of continental ones that have become part of everyday eating – like moussaka, bolognese sauce and stir-frys. In fact, despite the tradition of serving fish only on a Friday, there is no reason why it shouldn't appear almost every day of the week, even as Sunday lunch.

Chilli Fish 'n' Beans

If your family enjoy chilli-con-carne, try them on this fish version. It's low in fat, and just as delicious. Like most spicy dishes, it is even better if made the day before and then re-heated.

SERVES 4

2 tablespoons sunflower oil
1 onion, chopped
1 garlic clove, crushed
1 small green pepper, cored and chopped
400 g (14 oz) can of chopped or peeled tomatoes
415 g (14 oz) can of chilli beans, or red kidney beans with 1 teaspoon mild chilli powder added
a good pinch of ground cumin (optional)
1 teaspoon dried oregano
500 g (1 lb) white fish fillets, fresh or defrosted, skinned and cubed
salt and freshly ground black pepper

1. Heat the oil in a large saucepan and gently fry the onion, garlic and pepper for about 10 minutes.
2. Add the tomatoes and simmer for a further 10 minutes. Stir in the chilli beans, if using, otherwise add the kidney beans with the chilli powder. Add the cumin, if using, oregano and seasoning. Stir well, add the fish, and mix carefully to avoid breaking up the fish.
3. Cover and cook for another 10–12 minutes, until the fish is cooked. Serve hot, with grated cheese and crusty bread.

Top *Smoked Fish Gougère*, below *Chilli Fish 'n' Beans*

Smoked Fish Gougère

A gougère is a savoury choux pastry ring that rises while cooking; combined with fish it makes an attractive and tasty meal and yet it is not difficult to make.

SERVES 4

FOR THE CHOUX PASTRY
50 g (2 oz) butter, plus extra for greasing
150 ml (¼ pint) cold water
100 g (3½ oz) plain flour, sifted
3 eggs, beaten
75 g (3 oz) mature Cheddar cheese, grated
FOR THE FILLING
500 g (1 lb) smoked white fish fillets, fresh or defrosted, skinned, e.g. cod, haddock or whiting
600 ml (1 pint) milk
25 g (1 oz) butter or margarine
1 onion, chopped
50 g (2 oz) button mushrooms, sliced
1 teaspoon mild curry powder (optional)
50 g (2 oz) flour
25 g (1 oz) flaked almonds (optional)
salt and freshly ground black pepper

1. Preheat the oven to Gas Mark 6/200°C/400°F.
2. In a heavy-based saucepan, slowly melt the butter in the water and bring it to a rolling boil. Immediately draw off the boil and tip in all the flour at once. Beat well with a wooden spoon until the mixture forms a firm dough and leaves the side of the pan. Allow to cool for about 10 minutes.
3. When cooled, gradually mix in the eggs until the mixture stands in soft peaks. It may not be necessary to use all the eggs, so add them carefully. Stir in the cheese.
4. Spoon into a large, greased casserole dish, preferably not too high-sided. Make a well in the centre for the filling.
5. To make the filling: poach the fish in the milk, seasoning lightly. Remove the fish with a slotted spoon and flake the flesh, put the milk on one side.
6. In another saucepan, melt the butter or margarine and gently fry the onion and mushrooms for 5 minutes. Add the curry powder, if using, and fry for a minute; then stir in the flour.
7. Gradually blend in the reserved milk, stirring until thickened and smooth. Simmer for 2 minutes and then add the fish. Spoon into the centre of the choux ring, and scatter over the almonds, if using.
8. Bake for about 35 minutes, until the pastry has risen and is firm and crispy. Serve immediately.

Koulibiak – Russian Fish Pie

This is like a long fish pasty, and it only requires a small amount of white fish. This is combined with rice and eggs and then wrapped in crisp puff pastry. It is a good dish to make for a family party.

SERVES 4

FOR THE FILLING
25 g (1 oz) butter or margarine
1 small onion, chopped
3 tablespoons flour
150 ml (¼ pint) milk
2 tablespoons chopped fresh parsley
375 g (12 oz) white fish fillets, fresh or defrosted, skinned, cooked and flaked
50 g (2 oz) long grain rice, cooked
1 large egg (size 1–2), hard-boiled and chopped
1 tablespoon capers (optional)
salt and freshly ground black pepper
FOR THE PASTRY:
200 g (7 oz) packet of frozen puff pastry, defrosted
1 egg, beaten, to glaze
margarine, for greasing

1. Preheat the oven to Gas Mark 6/200°C/400°F.
2. Melt the butter or margarine and gently sauté the onion for 10 minutes. Stir in the flour and then gradually blend in the milk.
3. Season and add the parsley, cooked fish, rice, egg and capers, if using. Allow to cool.
4. Roll out the pastry to a large rectangle, until it is the thickness of a 10p piece. Place on a lightly greased baking sheet and brush round the edges with beaten egg.
5. Spoon the filling down the middle and draw up the pastry to the centre, pressing well to seal. Pinch to crimp the edges, making sure that the ends are well sealed. Glaze all over with the rest of the egg.
6. Bake for 25 minutes, until golden brown and crisp. Eat hot or warm, accompanied with peas or a salad.

Freddie Fish

This is a novelty fish pie, which younger children in particular will enjoy.

SERVES 4

350 g packet of frozen puff pastry, defrosted
25 g (1 oz) butter or margarine, plus extra for greasing
1 small onion, chopped
2 tablespoons flour, plus extra for rolling
200 ml (7 fl oz) semi-skimmed milk
250 g (8 oz) white fish fillets, fresh or defrosted, skinned and cut into bite-size pieces, e.g. cod, coley or haddock
175 g (6 oz) smoked white fish fillets, fresh or defrosted, skinned and cut into bite-size pieces
125 g (4 oz) frozen peas
2 slices of ham, cut in strips (optional)
a pinch of dried mixed herbs
1 egg, beaten, to glaze
salt and freshly ground black pepper

1. Preheat the oven to Gas Mark 6/200°C/400°F.
2. Roll out the pastry on a lightly floured board until it is approximately the thickness of a 10p piece. Cut in half and from the halves cut out two fish shapes. Do this by placing the halves on top of each other, so that the shapes match. Use the scraps to cut out small round discs for scales, re-rolling as necessary.
3. Place one fish shape on a lightly greased baking sheet.
4. Next, make the filling. Melt the butter or margarine and lightly sauté the onion for 10 minutes. Add the flour and the milk, stirring until smooth and thickened. Season well and add the fish. Cook gently for 10 minutes, until the fish is just cooked.
5. Add the peas and ham, if using, and simmer for another 3 minutes or so. Season and add the herbs. Allow the filling to cool.
6. Spoon the filling onto the pastry shape on the baking sheet, spreading almost to the edge. Brush the edges with some beaten egg and place the other pastry shape on top. Press well to seal and knock up and crimp with the back of a knife.
7. Lay the small discs of pastry on top, overlapping if liked. Using another scrap of pastry, make an eye. Glaze well all over with the beaten egg, pressing the scales of pastry lightly to the body.
8. Bake the pie for about 25 minutes, until golden brown and risen.

Top *Freddie Fish*, below *Granny's Sunday Visiting Fish*

Granny's Sunday Visiting Fish

Like most Grandmothers, I suspect, my Mother likes to give my children a good nourishing meal when they visit her, to 'feed them up'. This is her standard favourite, which is served with lots of lovely, creamy mashed potato. For really special visits, she makes little fish-shaped toasted croutons too!

SERVES 4

25 g (1 oz) butter or margarine
1 onion, chopped
2 medium-size carrots, grated
2 tablespoons cornflour
600 ml (1 pint) milk
1 large bay leaf
500 g (1 lb) white fish fillets, fresh or defrosted, skinned
grated rind of ½ and juice of 1 lemon
2 tablespoons chopped fresh parsley
salt and freshly ground black pepper

1. Melt the butter or margarine in a medium-size saucepan and gently sauté the onion and carrot for about 10 minutes.
2. Blend the cornflour with a little of the milk, and pour the rest of the milk into the saucepan. Bring to the boil; stir in the cornflour paste and stir until smooth and thickened. Add the bay leaf and simmer for 5 minutes.
3. Add the fish and simmer for 10 minutes, until cooked. Season.
4. Remove the bay leaf and add the lemon rind, lemon juice and parsley.
5. Keep warm until ready to serve, but do not let it bubble or it may curdle.

Note: to make fish-shaped croutons, cut out a fish-shaped template from paper. Using the template, cut out the shapes from white or brown bread with a small, sharp knife, allowing about 3 per person. Lightly toast and butter, or deep-fry until golden.

Vol-au-vent with Fish and Courgettes

This is a fish pie with a difference. Instead of the traditional oval shaped vol-au-vent, the pastry is cut into a fish shape and filled with a creamy fish and courgette mixture.

SERVES 4

350 g packet of frozen puff pastry, defrosted
1 egg, beaten, to glaze
FOR THE FILLING
750 g (1 ½ lb) white fish fillets, fresh or defrosted, skinned
600 ml (1 pint) fish or chicken stock
25 g (1 oz) butter or margarine
1 onion, chopped
2 carrots, grated
2 courgettes, sliced thinly
1 teaspoon ground coriander
grated rind and juice of 1 orange
125 g (4 oz) button mushrooms, sliced
2 tablespoons flour
4 tablespoons single cream or natural yogurt
salt and freshly ground black pepper

1. Preheat the oven to Gas Mark 6/200°C/400°F.
2. Roll out the pastry to a rectangle measuring about 23 × 28 cm (9 × 11 inches). Cut out a simple fish shape and place it on a baking sheet. Reserve any scraps.
3. With a small sharp knife, outline the fish shape 2.5 cm (1 inch) from the edge. Using scone cutters, cut out lots of fish scale shapes from the scraps, and cut out an eye for the fish too. Press these lightly onto the fish-shaped pastry.
4. Glaze the pastry all over with the beaten egg; then bake for 20–25 minutes. When golden brown and crisp, carefully lift off the top and scoop out the inside.
5. Meanwhile, make the filling. Poach the fish in the stock for about 10 minutes. Remove the fish and flake the flesh. Boil the stock down to 300 ml (½ pint).
6. Melt the butter or margarine in a saucepan and gently fry the onion, carrots and courgettes for about 10 minutes. Add the coriander, orange rind, orange juice and mushrooms and cook for 2 minutes.
7. Sprinkle in the flour, stir well and slowly add the reduced stock, stirring until thickened. Check the seasoning and return the fish; then stir in the cream or yogurt.
8. Spoon into the pastry case and serve immediately, topped with the pastry lid.

Italian-style Fried Fish

SERVES 4

4 large plaice, dab, megrim or sole fillets, fresh or defrosted, skinned
1 egg, beaten
75 g (3 oz) dried natural breadcrumbs
3 tablespoons grated parmesan cheese
1 teaspoon paprika
1 teaspoon dried oregano
sunflower oil, for frying
salt and freshly ground black pepper
1 lemon, quartered, to serve

1. Dip the fish in the beaten egg, making sure that it is well covered.
2. Mix together the breadcrumbs, cheese, paprika, oregano and seasoning. Shake out the mixture onto a plate. Dip the fish in the crumbs on both sides, pressing down well to coat evenly.
3. Pour enough oil into a pan to come to a depth of about 5 mm (¼ inch) and heat until it is quite hot. Fry the fish for about 3 minutes on each side. This may have to be done in two batches. Drain well on kitchen towel. Serve hot with the wedges of lemon.

Fish Turbans

SERVES 4

4 medium-size sole, plaice or witch fillets, fresh or defrosted, skinned
margarine, for greasing
125 g (4 oz) peeled prawns, fresh or defrosted
175 g (6 oz) cooked leaf spinach, drained and chopped roughly
150 g (5 oz) block of mozzarella cheese, or 125 g (4 oz) Edam cheese, grated
1 tablespoon chopped fresh parsley or chives
freshly grated nutmeg
salt and freshly ground black pepper

1. Preheat the oven to Gas Mark 5/190°C/375°F.
2. Cut each fillet in half lengthways and season. Lightly grease eight medium-size ramekins and roll the fillets round the edge.
3. Reserve 8 of the best prawns for garnish and chop the rest. Mix the chopped prawns with the spinach, cheese, and nutmeg.
4. Season and spoon the prawn mixture into the centre of each fish roll, piling it up if necessary.
5. Cover each ramekin with greased foil and place in a shallow roasting pan half-full of boiling water. Bake for about 25 minutes.
6. Allow to stand for a few minutes before turning out. Reserve any fish juices and mix with the parsley or chives to pour over the turbans when you serve them. Garnish with the reserved prawns.

CHEESY FISH AND MUSHROOM PANCAKES

Pancakes are always popular and they are a great way of encouraging children to eat fish. Although the recipe looks a little involved, the pancakes can always be made up in double quantity and frozen, interleaved with freezer film.

SERVES 4

FOR THE PANCAKES:
125 g (4 oz) plain flour, or 50 g (2 oz) each plain and wholemeal flours
a pinch of salt
1 egg
300 ml (½ pint) milk, preferably semi-skimmed
sunflower oil, for greasing
FOR THE FILLING:
25 g (1 oz) butter or margarine
1 small onion or large leek, sliced
2 tablespoons flour
300 ml (½ pint) milk
500 g (1 lb) white fish fillets, fresh or defrosted, skinned and cubed
1 bay leaf
a good pinch of ground mace or nutmeg
125 g (4 oz) button mushrooms, sliced
½ teaspoon dried mixed herbs
125 g (4 oz) Cheddar cheese, grated
½ packet of ready salted crisps, crushed roughly
salt and freshly ground black pepper

1. Preheat the oven to Gas Mark 6/200°C/400°F.
2. To make the pancakes: blend the flour, salt, egg and milk in a food processor until smooth. Alternatively, put the flour and salt in a large bowl and make a well in the centre. Drop in the egg and gradually beat in the flour, adding the milk slowly until you have a smooth batter.
3. Using a small frying pan, preferably non-stick, make about 8 pancakes, lightly brushing the base in between with oil. For successful, light and lacy pancakes, make sure the pan is nice and hot before you pour in the batter. Stack the pancakes on a plate, covering with a clean tea towel to keep pliable.
4. To make the filling: in a medium-size saucepan, melt the butter or margarine and gently fry the onion or leek for about 5 minutes, until softened. Stir in the flour and gradually work in the milk, stirring until blended.
5. Bring to the boil and add the fish, together with the bay leaf, mace or nutmeg and mushrooms. Season and simmer for 7 minutes. Add the herbs and half the cheese.
6. Lay the pancakes out and divide the filling between them. Roll up and lay in a greased, shallow ovenproof dish.

7. Scatter the remaining cheese and crisps on top and bake in the oven for about 15–20 minutes, until the top is crunchy and lightly browned.

FISH AND BROCCOLI CRUMBLE

Instead of a pie with a pastry top, try a savoury crumble instead. This is a good mid-week family meal, and it's easy to make.

SERVES 4

FOR THE FILLING:
3 tablespoons sunflower oil
1 onion, sliced
2 carrots, sliced
250 g (8 oz) broccoli
125 g (4 oz) button mushrooms, sliced
1 tablespoon flour
300 ml (½ pint) fish or chicken stock
250 g (8 oz) smoked white fish fillets, fresh or defrosted, skinned
250 g (8 oz) white fish fillets, fresh or defrosted, skinned
salt and freshly ground black pepper
FOR THE CRUMBLE TOPPING:
75 g (3 oz) plain flour
75 g (3 oz) wholemeal flour
75 g (3 oz) margarine or butter
75 g (3 oz) hard cheese, grated, e.g. Red Leicester

1. Preheat the oven to Gas Mark 5/190°C/375°F.
2. Heat the oil in a saucepan and gently sauté the onion and carrots for 5 minutes.
3. Slice the broccoli stalks into thin slices, reserving the florets, and add to the pan, along with the mushrooms. Fry these for another 5 minutes and then stir in the flour, followed by the stock and florets. Simmer for a further 5 minutes and season.
4. Put the fish into a medium-size casserole or pie dish and pour over the vegetables and stock. Stir gently to mix.
5. Next, make the topping. Rub the flours and fat together until they resemble fine breadcrumbs. Mix in the cheese.
6. Spoon the crumble over the fish mixture and level out the top. Bake for 35–40 minutes, until the top is lightly browned and the base bubbling. Serve hot, with boiled or baked potatoes.

Prawn Provençale

Treat your family to this tasty, simple dish. If you like prawns with a slightly sweet, meaty flavour, try and buy North Atlantic or cold-water prawns.

SERVES 4

175 g (6 oz) brown or white long grain rice
a little melted butter (optional)
2 tablespoons olive or sunflower oil
1 large onion, sliced
1 garlic clove, crushed
1 green pepper, cored and sliced
400 g (14 oz) can of chopped tomatoes
300 ml (½ pint) fish or chicken stock
1 teaspoon grated lemon rind
juice of 1 lemon
a small sprig of rosemary
250 g (8 oz) packet of frozen peeled prawns, defrosted
2 tablespoons chopped fresh parsley
salt and freshly ground black pepper

1. Boil the rice according to packet instructions. This may take 12 minutes for white rice and 30–40 minutes for brown. Drain, rinse in hot water and toss in a little melted butter, if wished.
2. Heat the oil and gently sauté the onion, garlic and pepper for about 5 minutes, until softened.
3. Add the tomatoes, stock, lemon rind and juice, rosemary and seasoning. Bring to the boil; then simmer for 10 minutes.
4. Add the prawns and cook for about 3 minutes, so that they are well heated through, but not overcooked and tough.
5. Sprinkle over the parsley and mix in gently. Serve with the rice.

Top *Prawn Provençale*, below *Creole Crab and Corn Pancakes*

Creole Crab and Corn Pancakes

These are delicious, lightly spiced, crab-filled pancakes covered in a tomato sauce. Use fresh, ready-prepared crab or buy a packet of frozen, mixing the brown and white meats together.

SERVES 4

8 pancakes (see p. 66)
FOR THE FILLING:
250 g (8 oz) prepared crab meat, fresh or defrosted
3 spring onions, chopped
1 tablespoon chilli relish
2 tablespoons mayonnaise
2 tablespoons soured cream
250 g (8 oz) sweetcorn, cooked if frozen
salt and freshly ground black pepper
oil, for greasing

FOR THE SAUCE:
2 tablespoons sunflower oil
1 onion, chopped
1 small green pepper, cored and chopped
1 garlic clove, crushed
400 g (14 oz) can of chopped tomatoes
150 ml (¼ pint) water or stock
½ teaspoon dried thyme
salt and freshly ground black pepper
50 g (2 oz) Cheddar cheese, grated, to serve

1. Preheat the oven to Gas Mark 5/190°C/375°F. Lay out the pancakes on a clean work surface.
2. Mix the crab with the rest of the filling ingredients, except for the oil, seasoning well.
3. Divide the filling between the pancakes. Roll or fold each one into four and place in a shallow, greased casserole dish.
4. To make the sauce: heat the sunflower oil and sauté the onion, pepper and garlic for 5 minutes. Add the tomatoes, water or stock, thyme and seasoning and simmer for 15 minutes.
5. Spoon the sauce over the pancakes and sprinkle the cheese over the top.
6. Heat through in the oven for 20 minutes, until the cheese has melted. Serve hot.

Flat Fish Rolls with Orangy Herb Stuffing

Ask your fishmonger to prepare the fish for you.

SERVES 4

125 g (4 oz) brown or white fresh breadcrumbs, plus 2 tablespoons to serve
1 small onion, grated
grated rind and juice of 1 orange
25 g (1 oz) butter, melted
½ teaspoon dried dill or thyme
2 tablespoons chopped fresh parsley
4 large or 8 small plaice, sole or dab fillets, fresh or defrosted, skinned
450 ml (¾ pint) fish or chicken stock
1 tablespoon cornflour
2 tablespoons water
3 tablespoons single cream or natural yogurt
50 g (2 oz) grated cheese
salt and freshly ground black pepper
orange slices, to garnish (optional)
watercress sprigs, to garnish (optional)

1. Preheat the oven to Gas Mark 4/180°C/350°F.
2. Mix the breadcrumbs with the onion, orange rind, half the orange juice, butter, herbs and seasoning.
3. Divide the filling between the fish fillets and roll up, securing each with a cocktail stick. Place join-side down in a shallow, ovenproof dish.
4. Mix the stock with the remaining orange juice and seasoning. Pour this over the fish, cover and bake for about 25 minutes, until cooked.
5. Drain the fish juices into a small saucepan, and bring to the boil.
6. Blend the cornflour with the water and mix it into the hot stock, stirring until smooth and thickened. Check the seasoning. Remove from the heat and stir in the cream or yogurt.
7. Arrange the rolls on a serving dish, pour over some of the sauce, and sprinkle with the cheese and breadcrumbs.
8. Flash quickly under the grill to brown and serve hot, garnished with the orange slices and watercress sprigs, if wished. Serve any leftover sauce separately.

Fish Steaks with Bacon and Cheese

This is one of my favourite quick, main-meal fish dishes.

SERVES 4

4 frozen fish steaks each weighing 100 g (3½ oz), defrosted
125 g (4 oz) hard cheese, e.g. Lancashire, Red Leicester or Cheddar
½ teaspoon dried thyme
4 large rashers of lean back bacon, de-rinded
a little sunflower oil
salt and freshly ground black pepper

1. Preheat the oven to Gas Mark 5/190°C/375°F. Season the fish.
2. Slice the cheese and lay half the slices on top of the fish steaks. Sprinkle with the thyme.
3. Wrap each steak in a bacon rasher, stretching slightly and keeping the join underneath.
4. Lay the 'parcels' in a lightly greased, shallow *gratin* dish and brush the bacon tops with a little oil. Bake for about 20–25 minutes. Halfway through the cooking time, lay the remaining cheese slices on top of each fish steak.

GRILLED FISH FILLETS WITH CUCUMBER SAUCE

Cucumber makes a very good fish sauce for any white fish.

SERVES 4

¼ cucumber, grated
4 white fish fillets, fresh or defrosted, each weighing about 175–250 g (6–8 oz), skinned
2 tablespoons sunflower or olive oil, or 25 g (1 oz) butter, melted
juice of 1 lemon
3–4 tablespoons mayonnaise
2 tablespoons soured cream or natural yogurt
1 tablespoon chopped fresh chives
1 teaspoon dried tarragon or ½ tablespoon chopped fresh mint (optional)
salt and freshly ground black pepper

1. Put the cucumber in a colander and sprinkle it lightly with salt. Leave to drain for 20 minutes or so.
2. Meanwhile, brush the fish with the oil or butter, season well and sprinkle with the lemon juice.
3. Grill for about 5 minutes each side for round fish, 3 minutes each side for flat. Baste with the pan juices when you turn the fish over.
4. Mix together the mayonnaise, cream or yogurt, herbs and seasoning. Drain the cucumber and pat it lightly with kitchen towel to dry; then mix it into the cream. Serve with the grilled fish.

Baked Mackerel with Tomato, Apple and Rosemary

The rich flesh of mackerel is nicely complemented by this light, fruity sauce. Herring is also delicious cooked this way.

SERVES 4

4 mackerel each weighing 250-375 g (8–12 oz), cleaned
1 small onion, sliced thinly
1 medium-size apple, cored and sliced
4 medium-size tomatoes, skinned and sliced
300 ml (½ pint) stock or water
a small sprig of fresh rosemary
butter, to dot (optional)
salt and freshly ground black pepper

1. Preheat the oven to Gas Mark 5/190°C/375°F.
2. Cut the heads from the fish, if liked. Wash the fish well and place in a shallow dish.
3. Put the onion, apple, tomatoes and stock or water in a saucepan with the rosemary and seasoning; cook for about 10 minutes.
4. Pour the sauce over the fish and dot with butter, if liked. Cover with foil and bake for about 20-25 minutes. Serve hot, or try it cold on a hot summer day!

Fish Plaki

Cod cutlets look the prettiest for this dish, but in fact any white fish fillets will do. A plaki is a favourite Greek dish.

SERVES 4

4 cutlets or white fish steaks, fresh or defrosted, each weighing 175 g (6 oz)
1 lemon, halved
2 tablespoons olive or sunflower oil
1 onion, sliced thinly
1 garlic clove, crushed
4 large ripe tomatoes, skinned and chopped
150 ml (¼ pint) water
a good pinch of dried dill
a good pinch of sugar
salt and freshly ground black pepper

1. Preheat the oven to Gas Mark 4/180°C/350°F.
2. Season the fish, lay it in a shallow baking dish, and squeeze over the juice from the lemon halves, taking care not to squash them too much. Slice the lemon halves afterwards.

3. Heat the oil in a saucepan and gently fry the onion and garlic for 5 minutes. Add the tomatoes, water, dill, sugar and seasoning. Simmer for 10 minutes; then spoon it over the fish.
4. Top with the slices of squeezed lemon and bake for about 40 minutes, until the fish is firm. Baste once or twice during cooking. Serve hot with rice, or cold with crusty bread and a salad.

Sunday Roast Monkfish

Instead of a joint, try a boneless, rolled monkfish tail. It can easily be carved in the same way. Use the juices to make gravy, or stir them into home-made tomato sauce to accompany the fish.

SERVES 4

1 large monkfish tail weighing about 1 kg (2 lb), filleted
2 tablespoons chopped fresh parsley
1 teaspoon dried thyme or a sprig of fresh thyme
juice of 1 lemon
2 garlic cloves, cut in slivers
butter, to dot
salt and freshly ground black pepper

1. Preheat the oven to Gas Mark 4/180°C/350°F.
2. Peel as much membrane off the fish as possible. Lay the two fillets at opposite ends to each other. Season, sprinkle over the herbs and half the lemon juice.
3. Lay the fillets on top of each other, wide end to tail end. Secure quite firmly with kitchen string.
4. Stab the top fillet in several places with a thin sharp knife and insert a sliver of garlic in each slash. Season, pour over the rest of the lemon juice, and dot with butter.
5. Place in a small roasting pan and roast for about 45 minutes, basting occasionally. Allow to stand for 5 minutes before carving into slices. Serve with potatoes and green vegetables.

MID-WEEK FISH STIR-FRY

A stir-fry is an excellent meal to prepare and cook if you're out at work, as the preparation can be done ahead and kept chilled until the evening. Make sure that everything is ready before cooking and then just quickly toss everything together.

SERVES 4

250 g (8 oz) chinese egg noodles
3 tablespoons light soy sauce
200 ml (7 fl oz) fish or chicken stock
2 teaspoons cornflour
a pinch of sugar
375 g (12 oz) white fish fillets, fresh or defrosted, skinned and cut into bite-size pieces, e.g. cod, haddock or monkfish
4 tablespoons sunflower oil, plus a little extra
3 spring onions, sliced thinly
1 garlic clove, chopped
2.5 cm (1-inch) cube of fresh ginger, grated
2 carrots, cut in thin sticks
2 celery sticks, sliced thinly
1 small green pepper, cored and sliced thinly
50 g (2 oz) chinese leaves or cabbage, sliced thinly
50 g (2 oz) beanshoots
125 g (4 oz) peeled prawns, fresh or defrosted (optional)
salt and freshly ground black pepper

1. Soak the noodles in boiling water, according to packet instructions. Drain and toss in a little oil, ideally a few drops of sesame oil if you have any.
2. Mix the soy sauce, stock, cornflour and sugar in a cup. Season the fish.
3. Heat 2 tablespoons of the oil in a wok or large frying pan. Carefully fry the fish in the hot oil for just a few minutes until cooked, taking care not to break up the fish too much. Remove with a slotted spoon.
4. Add 2 more tablespoons of oil to the wok and stir-fry the onions, garlic, ginger, carrots, celery and pepper for 3 minutes; then toss in the chinese leaves or cabbage, beanshoots and prawns.
5. Pour in the sauce, stirring until the mixture thickens. Return the fish, stirring lightly. Serve immediately with the noodles.

Top *Mid-week Fish Stir-fry*, below *Fish Balls Bolognese*

Fish Balls Bolognese

This is a great hit with my children: they enjoy rolling the fish into balls and they find it easy to eat, without any worry about bones. Even my virtually vegetarian younger daughter asks for more.

SERVES 4

250 g (8 oz) spaghetti
FOR THE FISH BALLS:
500 g (1 lb) white fish fillets, fresh or defrosted, skinned
1 small onion, chopped
2 tablespoons chopped fresh parsley or ½ teaspoon dried marjoram
salt and freshly ground black pepper
FOR THE SAUCE:
2 tablespoons sunflower oil
1 small onion, chopped
2 celery sticks, chopped
2 carrots, chopped
1 garlic clove, crushed
½ teaspoon dried marjoram
500 g carton of creamed tomatoes or 400 g (14 oz) can of tomatoes
2 tablespoons tomato purée
300 ml (½ pint) fish or chicken stock
salt and freshly ground black pepper
grated parmesan cheese, to serve

1. Boil the spaghetti according to packet instructions; drain and keep warm.
2. To make the fish balls: put the fish, onion, herbs and seasoning into a food processor and blend to a fairly smooth pulp. This can be done in a blender, but it is less easy and may have to be carried out in batches.
3. With wet hands, shape the fish mixture into about 16 small balls and place on a plate.
4. To make the sauce: heat the oil in a large saucepan and gently sauté the onion, celery, carrots and garlic for about 10 minutes, until softened.
5. Add the herbs, tomatoes, tomato purée, stock and seasoning. Bring to the boil and then turn down to simmer, for about 5 minutes.
6. Drop the fish balls into the sauce; cover and simmer for 10 more minutes, until cooked.
7. Serve hot with the spaghetti and grated parmesan cheese.

Fish and Pasta Shapes in Spinach Sauce

This is a super main-meal dish: it is full of protein and fibre, and rich in iron and vitamins. It tastes good too.

SERVES 4

250 g (8 oz) pasta shapes
25 g (1 oz) butter or margarine
1 onion, chopped
2 celery sticks, chopped
2 tablespoons flour
600 ml (1 pint) milk
250 g (8 oz) frozen leaf spinach, defrosted
500 g (1 lb) smoked or white fish fillets, fresh or defrosted, skinned and diced, e.g. cod, haddock or coley
freshly grated nutmeg
salt and freshly ground black pepper
50–75 g (2–3 oz) cheese, grated, to serve

1. Boil the pasta according to packet instructions; then drain. Put on one side.
2. Melt the butter or margarine and gently fry the onion and celery for about 2 minutes, until softened. Stir in the flour and then blend in the milk, until smooth and thickened.
3. Drain the spinach, squeezing out any excess liquid, and add it to the sauce. Season with the nutmeg, to taste, and salt and pepper.
4. Simmer the sauce for a few minutes, add the fish, and cook for about 10 minutes.
5. Add the pasta and heat through.
6. Serve hot, sprinkled with the grated cheese.

USING READY-PREPARED FISH

Now that so much fish is sold fully skinned and filleted, there is little need to pre-cook fish in many dishes in order to skin and bone it. Instead, simply chop and use as required.

Aubergine and Fish Moussaka

This is another family favourite which adapts well to fish instead of meat; it is also quicker to cook.

SERVES 4

1 medium-size aubergine, sliced
8–10 tablespoons sunflower oil
1 onion, chopped
1 large potato, diced
1 garlic clove, crushed
400 g (14 oz) can of peeled or chopped tomatoes
1 teaspoon dried marjoram or oregano
1–2 tablespoons chopped fresh parsley
500 g (1 lb) white fish fillets, fresh or defrosted, skinned and cubed
salt and freshly ground black pepper
FOR THE SAUCE:
25 g (1 oz) butter or margarine
2 tablespoons flour
450 ml (¾ pint) milk
1 egg, beaten
75 g (3 oz) mature Cheddar cheese, grated
salt and freshly ground black pepper

1. Preheat the oven to Gas Mark 5/190°C/375°F.
2. Layer the aubergine slices in a colander and sprinkle them lightly with salt. Leave to drain for 30 minutes over a sink. Rinse well and pat dry with kitchen towel.
3. Meanwhile, make the fish base. Heat 2 tablespoons of the oil in a large saucepan and gently fry the onion, potato and garlic for about 10 minutes, until softened.
4. Add the tomatoes, herbs and seasoning. Simmer for 10 minutes and then carefully mix in the fish. Spoon into the base of a medium-size casserole dish.
5. Heat half the remaining oil in a frying pan and fry half the aubergine slices. Use the remaining oil to fry the rest of the aubergine. If you wish to cut down on the oil, cover the pan as you fry: the steam will help cook the slices. Arrange the aubergines on top of the fish.
6. Now make the sauce. Put the butter or margarine, flour and milk into another saucepan and bring slowly to the boil, stirring, until thickened and smooth. Simmer for about 2 minutes and season.
7. Remove the sauce from the heat and mix in the beaten egg and two-thirds of the cheese. Pour this over the aubergine layer and sprinkle over the last of the cheese.
8. Bake the moussaka for about 25–30 minutes, until golden brown and bubbling. Serve hot with crusty sesame seed bread and a simple, Greek-style cucumber and tomato salad.

Super Fish Pie

Everyone loves a good fish pie! This one is ideal for a special family meal; don't worry about the cider for children, as the alcohol bubbles away during cooking. If you like, use a more economical species of fish, such as coley, but don't skimp on the prawns!

SERVES 4

FOR THE TOPPING:
750 g (1 ½ lb) potatoes
a good knob of butter
a pinch of freshly grated nutmeg
salt and freshly ground black pepper
FOR THE FILLING:
25 g (1 oz) butter
1 onion, chopped
3 tablespoons flour
150 ml (¼ pint) dry cider (optional)
450 ml (¾ pint) fish or chicken stock
3 tablespoons single or double cream
2 tomatoes, skinned and quartered
125 g (4 oz) button mushrooms, halved if large
500 g (1 lb) white fish fillets, fresh or defrosted, skinned, e.g. cod, coley or haddock
250 g (8 oz) peeled prawns, fresh or defrosted
2 tablespoons chopped fresh parsley
juice of ½ lemon
2 tablespoons chopped mixed nuts, or ½ packet of crisps, crushed
salt and freshly ground black pepper

1. Preheat the oven to Gas Mark 6/200°C/400°F.
2. Boil the potatoes in lightly salted water, until just tender. Drain well, return to the saucepan and heat for a few minutes, shaking the pan occasionally to dry the potatoes well. Mash with the butter, seasoning and nutmeg.
3. Meanwhile, make the filling. Melt the butter in a large saucepan and gently fry the onion for about 5 minutes, until softened. Stir in the flour and then gradually add the cider, if using, and stock. Add the cream.
4. Stir in the tomatoes and mushrooms. Season and simmer for 5–6 minutes.
5. Add the fish and prawns; then stir in the parsley and lemon juice.
6. Spoon the filling into a 1.2 litre (2-pint) pie dish and either spoon or pipe the potato on top. Sprinkle over the nuts or crisps and bake for 20 minutes, until the top is brown and bubbling.

Two Fish and Bean Cassoulet

A cassoulet is a traditional French peasant dish made with mixed meat and beans. Fish can be substituted for an equally delicious, highly nutritious meal. This makes a large quantity, so freeze half for later if you can't eat it all at once.

SERVES 4

500 g (1 lb) smoked fish fillets, fresh or defrosted, skinned
500 g (1 lb) white fish fillets, fresh or defrosted, skinned, e.g. monkfish, hake or coley
3 tablespoons sunflower oil
1 large onion, sliced
1 garlic clove, crushed
2 carrots, sliced
4 rashers of lean streaky bacon, de-rinded and chopped
900 ml (1 ½ pints) fish or chicken stock
400 g (14 oz) can of tomatoes
a good pinch of ground mace or nutmeg
½ teaspoon dried thyme or mixed herbs
a small sprig of rosemary (optional)
1 bay leaf
425 g can of haricot or cannellini (white kidney) beans
salt and freshly ground black pepper
3 tablespoons dried breadcrumbs, to serve (optional)
2 tablespoons chopped fresh parsley, to serve (optional)

1. Cut the fish into bite-size chunks, checking for pin bones, and reserve.
2. In a large flameproof casserole or saucepan, heat the oil and gently sauté the onion, garlic and carrot with the bacon for about 10 minutes, until softened.
3. Add the stock, tomatoes, spice, herbs and some seasoning. Bring to the boil and add the fish. Cover and simmer for 10 minutes.
4. Uncover, add the beans with their liquor, and re-heat for about 5 minutes.
5. If you wish to serve the cassoulet in the traditional way, spoon it into a shallow dish. Sprinkle over the breadcrumbs and the parsley and lightly brown under the grill.
6. Serve immediately, with crusty bread and green beans.

Stuffed Tomatoes with Celery and Fish

These are delicious served with potatoes or pasta and accompanied by watercress.

SERVES 4

25 g (1 oz) butter or margarine
1 onion, chopped
1 garlic clove, crushed (optional)
2 celery sticks, chopped
4 beef tomatoes or 8 large round tomatoes
250 g (8 oz) cooked brown rice
1 large 'hot' smoked mackerel fillet, skinned and flaked
1 teaspoon horseradish relish (optional)
½ teaspoon dried mixed herbs
salt and freshly ground black pepper

1. Preheat the oven to Gas Mark 6/200°C/400°F.
2. Melt the butter or margarine and gently fry the onion, garlic, if using, and celery for 10 minutes.
3. Slice the tops off the tomatoes and scoop out the flesh, reserving the shells. Add the flesh to the pan and cook for about 5 minutes.
4. Stir in the cooked rice, flaked mackerel, relish, if using, and herbs. Check the seasoning, it may not need any.
5. Pile the mixture into the tomato shells, replace the tops, and place in a shallow casserole dish.
6. Bake for about 15–20 minutes, until the tomatoes are just softened and the filling is quite hot.

Fish Dishes From Other Lands

All over the world, people in different countries have tasty and exciting ways of cooking fish. Whilst we may not be able to buy some of their more unusual fish, we can still use their ideas, because fish is so versatile.

Seafish Paella

A paella is always a special meal in Spain, in fact anywhere in the Mediterranean. Try it for a special weekend family meal.

SERVES 4

3 tablespoons sunflower or olive oil
250 g (8 oz) filleted monkfish, fresh or defrosted, cubed
2 red mullets each weighing about 175 g (6 oz) (optional)
250 g (8 oz) white fish fillets, fresh or defrosted, skinned and cubed
250 g (8 oz) large prawns in their shells, fresh or defrosted
2 garlic cloves, crushed
1 teaspoon paprika
a pinch of dried rosemary
1 onion, chopped
400 g (14 oz) can of chopped tomatoes
250 g (8 oz) risotto or long grain rice
600 ml (1 pint) fish, chicken or vegetable stock
a pinch of saffron threads, soaked in a little warm water
salt and freshly ground black pepper
2 tablespoons chopped fresh parsley, to garnish

1. Heat the oil in a large frying pan and fry the monkfish for 3 minutes.
2. Remove the heads from the mullets and then halve the bodies. Add these to the pan together with the white fish and the prawns. Fry for about 5 more minutes, stirring carefully now and again, until cooked. Remove the fish with a slotted spoon and keep covered.
3. Add the garlic, paprika, rosemary and onion to the pan and sauté for 5 minutes.
4. Stir in the tomatoes, rice, stock and saffron, with its water. Season, bring to the boil, partially cover and simmer for about 15–20 minutes, stirring once or twice. If the mixture looks as if it is drying out too quickly, add extra water: it should be quite creamy.
5. Return the fish, stirring it in carefully, and check the seasoning. Sprinkle with the parsley and serve immediately.

Top *Bouillabaisse*, below *Seafish Paella*

Bouillabaisse

This traditional fish soup originates in the South of France, where it normally contains many fish species that are not easily available over here. However, the beauty of this recipe is that it is easily adapted to fish from these shores. But it is important to use a good olive oil if the essential flavour is to be retained.

SERVES 4

6 tablespoons olive oil
1 onion, chopped
1 large leek, sliced
1 small fennel bulb, sliced
2 garlic cloves, crushed
6 ripe tomatoes, skinned and chopped
a bouquet garni
1 large bay leaf
3 strips of orange peel
a good pinch of saffron threads
1.5 litres (2½ pints) fish or chicken stock, or water
750 g (1½ lb) mixed fish fillets, fresh or defrosted, skinned and cut into large bite-size pieces, e.g. conger eel, mackerel, coley, whiting, red mullet and monkfish
250 g (8 oz) large prawns in their shells, fresh or defrosted (optional)
salt and freshly ground black pepper
2 tablespoons chopped fresh parsley, to garnish

1. Heat half the oil in a large saucepan and gently sauté the onion, leek, fennel and garlic for 10 minutes.
2. Add the tomatoes, herbs and orange peel, and crumble in the saffron. Pour in the remaining oil and add the stock. Season and bring to a rapid boil to mix the oil and stock thoroughly. This is important if the oil is not to float on the top.
3. Reduce the heat to a moderate simmer and cook for 5 minutes.
4. Add the fish in stages to ensure even cooking. The firmer fleshed fish, such as monkfish and conger eel, should be added first, followed by the more flaky fish, such as whiting. This should be done at about 5-minute intervals, until just cooked. Then lift the fish out with a slotted spoon and keep warm. Finally, add the prawns, if using, and cook for about 3 minutes.
5. To serve: first eat the liquor as a light soup poured into soup bowls over slices of toasted French bread. Then sprinkle the fish and vegetables with the parsley and serve accompanied with hot, boiled potatoes and garlic-flavoured mayonnaise.

Indian Fish Korma

Fish and curry spices go marvellously together and because this is a mild, gentle dish, it is a good way of introducing your children to curry. The flavour is even better if it is made the day before and then re-heated.

SERVES 4

2 tablespoons desiccated coconut
450 ml (3/4 pint) boiling water
25 g (1 oz) butter
1 tablespoon oil
1 onion, chopped
2 carrots, sliced thinly
1–2 garlic cloves, crushed
250 g (8 oz) potato, sliced
2.5 cm (1-inch) cube of fresh ginger, grated, or 1 teaspoon ground ginger
1 fresh green chilli, de-seeded and chopped (optional)
2 teaspoons ground coriander
1 teaspoon ground cumin
2 teaspoons ground turmeric
1/2 teaspoon ground cinnamon
2 whole cloves
4 white fish fillets, fresh or defrosted, each weighing 250 g (8 oz), skinned, e.g. cod, haddock, coley or whiting
125 g (4 oz) frozen peas
2 tablespoons cream or natural yogurt
salt and freshly ground black pepper

1. Soak the coconut in the boiling water for 20 minutes. Strain, pressing out as much liquid from the coconut as possible, and discard the coconut.
2. Heat the butter and oil and sauté the onion, carrots, garlic and potato for 10 minutes, until softened. Add the ginger, the chilli, if using, and the rest of the spices. Fry for a minute or two.
3. Pour in the coconut water, bring to the boil and simmer for 5 minutes. Add the fish and spoon the sauce over. Season, cover and cook gently for another 12–15 minutes.
4. With a slotted spoon, transfer the fish and the vegetables to a serving plate and keep warm in a low oven. Add the peas to the sauce. Bubble the sauce until it is reduced to about half the quantity and then remove from the heat.
5. Stir in the cream or yogurt and spoon or pour the sauce over the fish and vegetables. Serve hot with rice.

Cantonese Sweet and Sour Fish

Chinese food is very popular with children, as it is tasty without being too hot and spicy. My children particularly enjoy this way of cooking fish and it is easy to eat as well as colourful to look at. Serve with rice or noodles for a delicious meal.

SERVES 4

1 egg white
2 tablespoons cornflour
1 tablespoon soy sauce
1 teaspoon five spice powder (optional)
500 g (1 lb) white flat fish fillets, fresh or defrosted, skinned and sliced in thick strips
oil, for deep-fat frying
1 medium-size leek, sliced diagonally, or 4 spring onions, sliced
1 garlic clove, crushed
1 red pepper, cored and sliced
¼ cucumber, halved, de-seeded and sliced
1 tablespoon grated fresh ginger or 1 teaspoon ground ginger

FOR THE SAUCE:
4 tablespoons pineapple or apple juice
2 tablespoons medium-dry sherry (optional)
2 tablespoons wine vinegar
2 teaspoons sugar
1 tablespoon soy sauce
150 ml (¼ pint) water
1 tablespoon cornflour
salt (optional)
freshly ground black pepper

1. Mix all the sauce ingredients in a jug and keep on one side.
2. Mix the egg white, cornflour, soy sauce and spice powder in a bowl and mix in the fish strips.
3. Heat about 2.5 cm (1 inch) of oil in a wok or heavy, deep frying pan, until it is quite hot. Add the fish, stir-frying for about 2 minutes until it is golden brown and crispy. Remove the fish with a slotted spoon and drain on kitchen towel. Keep it warm, uncovered, in a low oven.
4. Pour off all but 2 tablespoons of the oil and re-heat. Stir-fry all the vegetables, together with the ginger, for 3 minutes until they are just cooked but still crisp.
5. Pour the sauce over the vegetables and stir until it has thickened. Taste for seasoning – it may not need extra salt.
6. Spoon the sauce over the fish and serve immediately so that the fish is still quite crispy.

Top *Cantonese Sweet and Sour Fish*, below *Cod Portugaise*

Cod Portugaise

The Portuguese are great fish eaters, situated as they are right on the rich Atlantic sea board. One of their favourite fish is cod, but you can use any round white fish in this recipe if you prefer.

SERVES 4

2 tablespoons oil, preferably olive oil
1 onion, sliced
1 garlic clove, crushed (optional)
1 green pepper, cored and sliced
400 g (14 oz) can of chopped tomatoes
1 teaspoon paprika
grated rind and juice of 1 orange
4 cod fillets or other white fish fillets, fresh or defrosted, each weighing about 175–250 g (6–8 oz), skinned
salt and freshly ground black pepper
1 tablespoon chopped fresh parsley or coriander, to garnish

1. Heat the oil and sauté the onion, garlic and pepper for about 5 minutes, until softened.
2. Add the tomatoes, paprika and orange juice. Season, stir well and simmer for a further 5 minutes.
3. Lay the fish fillets on top, cutting them to fit the pan if necessary. Season lightly, cover and simmer gently for 12–15 minutes, or until the fish is cooked but still firm. Serve hot, sprinkled with the parsley or coriander and the orange rind.

Balchi di Pisca – Mexican Fish Balls

MAKES 16–20 BALLS

500 g (1 lb) filleted white fish, fresh or defrosted, skinned, or 5 frozen fish steaks each weighing 90 g, defrosted
125 g (4 oz) fresh white breadcrumbs
2 tablespoons mild chilli relish
1 teaspoon ground cumin (optional)
2 tablespoons chopped fresh coriander or parsley
75 g (3 oz) natural dried breadcrumbs
oil, for deep-frying
salt and freshly ground black pepper

1. Mince or process the fish in a food processor until blended but not too smooth.
2. Mix this with all the other ingredients, except for the dried breadcrumbs and the oil.
3. Divide the mixture into small balls the size of an egg; roll these until smooth and toss them in the dried breadcrumbs.

4. Meanwhile, half-fill a deep-fat frying pan with oil. Heat to a temperature of 180°C/350°F, or until hot enough to brown a cube of day-old bread in a minute. Deep-fry the balls in two or three batches for about 5 minutes. Remember to re-heat the oil between batches so that the outsides seal well.
5. Drain on kitchen towel and serve hot and crispy.

Scandinavian Herring

The Scandinavians are very fond of herring and they have many different ways of preparing it. This particular dish is ideal for a tasty supper. It is best served with green vegetables and plain boiled potatoes.

SERVES 4

4 large herring each weighing about 375 g (12 oz), cleaned and boned with the tails left on
1–2 teaspoons coarse-grain mustard
1 tablespoon tomato purée
2 tablespoons single cream
a pinch of dried mixed herbs or dried dill weed
25 g (1 oz) butter or margarine, melted
salt and freshly ground black pepper
fresh lemon wedges, to garnish

1. Make a small slit in the skin of each herring, where the back fins were. Preheat the oven to Gas Mark 4/180°C/350°F.
2. Mix together the mustard, purée, cream, herbs and seasoning and spread this on the flesh side of the fish.
3. Roll up and push the tails through the slit and secure each with a cocktail stick. Place join-side down in a baking dish, and brush with the melted butter or margarine.
4. Bake, uncovered, for 25 minutes. Serve hot, garnished with the lemon slices.

SQUID FRITTO MISTO DE MARE

Fritto Misto de Mare is a popular Italian dish simply consisting of morsels of crisply fried fish. One of the best fish to use is squid and children are actually quite fond of it as it is mild and boneless. It is delicious served with a bowl of garlic-flavoured mayonnaise or tomato ketchup.

SERVES 4–6

750 g (1 ½ lb) squid, prepared and sliced in rings
50 g (2 oz) plain flour
1 teaspoon dried oregano
sunflower oil, for deep-frying
salt and freshly ground black pepper
fresh lemon wedges, to serve

1. Wash the prepared squid rings and tentacles well and drain.
2. Mix together the flour, oregano and seasoning. Toss the squid rings in this until they are well coated.
3. Heat enough oil to half-fill a deep-fat frying pan to a temperature of 185°C/360°F, or until a cube of day-old bread browns in about 30 seconds. Deep-fry the squid in batches for about 3 minutes at a time, returning the oil to temperature between batches.
4. Drain on kitchen towel and serve hot as soon as possible, with the lemon wedges.

Note: To prepare squid
If your fishmonger doesn't sell ready-prepared squid, follow these instructions. Pull the head and tentacles off the squid and pull out the transparent bone. Discard this, along with the insides. Cut the tentacles off just below the eyes and discard the head. Peel the membrane off and wash the squid thoroughly, inside and out. Finally, slice diagonally into rings.

Moroccan Fish Tagine

A *tagine* is a conical cooking pot with a sealed lid; it is a traditional cooking method used in North Africa. The shape of the pot allows the steam to trickle back down onto the food, thus keeping it moist while it is cooking gently. It is used for cooking meat or fish with vegetables and a wide variety of herbs and spices. This is a tasty but simple fish tagine.

SERVES 4

750 g (1 ½ lb) white fish fillets, fresh or defrosted, skinned and cut into large chunks
juice of 1 lemon
4 tablespoons chopped fresh parsley
1 teaspoon paprika
1 teaspoon ground cumin (optional)
1 garlic clove, crushed
3 tablespoons sunflower or olive oil
1 onion, sliced
4 celery sticks, cut into chunks
2 carrots, sliced thickly
2 medium-size potatoes, sliced thickly
400 g (14 oz) can of chopped tomatoes
150 ml (¼ pint) water
2 courgettes, cut into large chunks
salt and freshly ground black pepper

1. Place the fish in a wide, shallow dish. Mix the lemon juice with the parsley, paprika, cumin, if using, and garlic; use a food processor or blender if preferred.
2. Pour this over the fish and rub it well in. Leave the fish to marinate for at least 30 minutes, preferably more.
3. Heat the oil in a large cast-iron or heavy-based saucepan with a tightly fitting lid. Gently sauté the onion, celery, carrots and potatoes for about 10 minutes.
4. Add the tomatoes, water, courgettes and seasoning. Bring to the boil, cover and simmer for 15 minutes.
5. Remove the fish and pour the marinade juices into the vegetable sauce, stirring well in. Lay the fish on top of this, scraping any remaining marinade onto the top.
6. Return the lid, making sure that it is on tightly, and continue to simmer gently for 10–15 minutes, depending on the thickness of the fish. Serve with boiled rice or traditional steamed couscous, which many supermarkets now stock.

Greek Taramasalata

More local fishmongers are selling smoked cod's roe now, but don't be put off by the high price – a little goes a long way, and this dish is quickly made in a food processor or blender.

SERVES 4

2 large slices of white bread, crusts removed
125 g (4 oz) smoked cod's roe
1–2 garlic cloves, chopped roughly
juice of ½ lemon
150 ml (¼ pint) olive oil, plus extra for garnishing
freshly ground black pepper
black olives, to garnish

1. Soak the bread briefly in enough cold water to cover, and squeeze lightly.
2. Put into a processor or blender with the roe, garlic, lemon and oil. Season with a few turns of ground black pepper, although no salt should be necessary. Blend until it is smooth, scraping down the sides. If it looks too thick, add extra cold water.
3. Spoon into a bowl and chill until required.
4. To serve it the traditional way: swirl the top, trickle over a little olive oil and garnish with black olives. Accompany with fingers of pitta bread, sesame bread sticks or fresh vegetable sticks.

INDEX

Design: Sue Storey
Illustrations: Clare Newbolt
Photography: Clive Streeter
Styling: Sue Russel
Food preparation for photography: Lyn Rutherford
Typesetting: Goodfellow & Egan, Cambridge
Printed and bound in Spain by Cayfosa, Barcelona